Exploring

HAWAII

Your Complete Guide to Oahu and the Big Island's Best Beaches, Volcanoes, and Adventures

Paul Toader

Table of Contents

INTRODUCTION

Welcome (maybe again) to Hawaii! It brings me so much joy to go through all of this trouble to wish you (and give you the information you need) about this sand-covered speck in the Pacific. Honestly, my three long weeks in Hawaii in November were some of the best of my life. I'm sure you will enjoy the island as much as I did. You can road trip it (3 hr drive maximum distance any-which-way), strike out into the Na Pali, snorkel in Waimea, and kayak (oops, no kayaking) in Hanalei. You can see cafes in Hanapepe and sip sun-warmed rum at the Kōloa Rum Co. just up the hill.

The locals and locals-only appreciate the "mystique" of Hawaii and oftentimes don't enjoy the ruddy intrusion of tourists, which always makes one feel very chuffed to be surrounded by them in a swimsuit at the otherwise pristine beaches. Something else about the island: first of all, I need to use the proper word to talk about Kaua'i! Hawaiians consider that word to be very connected to European colonialism and the manipulation of the sugar plantation economy.

In Oahu, there are only a couple of towns – quite a few living in cities and suburbs, very close to the countryside. It gives the island a feeling of peacefulness that I always associate with Bob Ross and not much else. I caught at least seven eggs sitting in my tent cooking dinner one night, and poor chickens are getting killed in crosswalks. Pretty much tame! Oahu'ians are welcoming, as much as to say that not all will welcome you graciously.

Welcome to Hawaii

Hey there! Pardon me for eavesdropping, but I've gathered that you might be Hawaii-bound. I don't like to start off with the hard sell, you know, but let me try to whet your appetite with a little bit of information. It is I, the author, and I'll be your faithful guide, leading you on a virtual exploration of the islands from the comfort of your own home. Speaking of comfort, isn't it more wonderful to travel far and wide knowing there's a place to call your own? For some of us, the open road knows no bounds; stepping out the door, with a backpack stuffed full and pockets a bit light, signaling the beginnings of the next great adventure. Yet now and again, even a wandering soul resuscitates the spirit with a bit of rest and relaxation. Rest and relaxation, a strange and wondrously rare pair of words that just go well together. One might suggest that they're the perfect candidates for their shared piece of lexical real estate: the alliteration just works!

But abstractions aside, there are few bits of advice that travelers around the world can exchange. "Go to Hawaii," however, is one of them. Who doesn't keep Hawaii tucked away as one of those picturesque "one day" trips? Gentle climate, gin-clear waters, green palms waving in the balmy breeze - it's half artificial in its timelessness these days, a postcard island as kickoff party for the new century. And yet that's just about all that's been said. There's no handbook for Hawaii, no template anyone steers by once they've popped the champagne and unloaded the luau. Deep in the stretch of paradise they are vigorously working on the tomorrow of runs and rugby, of cyclists and surfers, of sun-kissed skilled workers walking to their sustainable friend's organic barista shop. They're designing it, one year at a time.

Brief History and Facts About Hawaii

Ever wonder why volcanoes often feature prominently in Hawaii's photography? That's because the isles were actually created by numerous undersea volcanoes emerging from the ocean floor. The Hawaiian Heritage is an outstanding thing as well! As far as geography, the Hawaiian Islands' crucial characteristics are its a dozen islands, its developing third-furthest nautical point worldwide from any landmass, as well as its status as the smallest landlocked state. Hawaii had been ruled by the native sovereign who maintained the Midnight Ceremony prior to Westerners setting foot on the state, a time for touching noses. In 1900, the territory formally joined the U.S. as a part of the Hawaiian Islands.

Hawaii, located in the central Pacific Ocean about 2,100 miles southwest of the continental United States, is the only island state in the United States. The word "Hawaii" is taken largely from the Polynesian word "Havaii" which means homeland. It employs the loved nickname "The Aloha State" in good faith. In Hawaiian, "aloha" is used for

both "hello" and "farewell". The composed melody for the state was "'Hawai'i Pono'i" which means "Hawaii's Own" in Hawaiian. Hawaii got its name from the traditional word "Hawaiki" which is understood to be the historical land. Its capital and largest municipality is Honolulu located on the isle of Oahu. The state's economy is based greatly on tourism, agriculture, fisheries, and of course, ecology.

Hilton Hawaiian Village

CHAPTER 1: GETTING TO AND AROUND HAWAII: YOUR ISLAND TRANSPORTATION GUIDE

Assuming you're already in Hawaii, here are your traveling options, but remember distances and travel times between points of interest in your islands greatly vary; all figures are approximate.

If visiting more than one island, you may combine various modes of travel on a single ticket, cheaper than purchasing separate tickets. You may also purchase passes which discount the cost of inter-island flights.

Getting to Hawaii

Choosing Your Flights

Flying into Honolulu or Kona/Hilo requires careful consideration of airlines, flight experiences, baggage policies, and airport amenities. Below is a detailed guide to help you navigate your travel to Oahu and the Big Island.

Flying into Honolulu (Oahu)

Major Airlines and Smaller Carriers:

1 **Hawaiian Airlines**

Description:

Hawaiian Airlines is Hawaii's largest and longest-serving airline. Travelers can expect a taste of Hawaiian hospitality with complimentary meals and drinks, in-flight entertainment, and comfortable seating.

Pros:
- Complimentary meals and beverages on all flights.
- Extensive network with many direct flights to and from the U.S. mainland.
- Hawaiian-themed in-flight entertainment and amenities.

Cons:
- Higher ticket prices compared to some competitors.
- Limited baggage allowance in basic economy fare.

Typical Flight Duration:
- Los Angeles to Honolulu: Approximately 5 hours and 50 minutes.
- New York to Honolulu: Approximately 11 hours.

Baggage Allowance:
- Main Cabin Basic: One personal item; no checked baggage included.
- Main Cabin: One personal item, one carry-on, and one checked bag.
- First Class: Two checked bags included.

Airport Amenities:
- Restaurants: Local and international cuisine options.
- Shops: Duty-free stores, local crafts, and souvenirs.
- Services: Currency exchange, ATMs, car rental services, and lounges.

How to Book:
- 🌐 **Website:** https://www.hawaiianairlines.com
- ☎ **Phone:** 1-800-367-5320

2) United Airlines
📝 **Description:**
United Airlines offers a broad network of flights to Honolulu with a range of service classes from Basic Economy to Polaris Business Class. Travelers can expect reliable service and extensive connectivity.

Pros:
- Numerous direct and connecting flights from various U.S. cities.
- MileagePlus loyalty program benefits.
- In-flight Wi-Fi and entertainment options.

Cons:
- Basic Economy fare has limited amenities.
- Potential for additional fees for seat selection and checked bags.

Typical Flight Duration:
- San Francisco to Honolulu: Approximately 5 hours and 30 minutes.
- Chicago to Honolulu: Approximately 9 hours.

Baggage Allowance:
- Basic Economy: One personal item only.
- Economy: One personal item, one carry-on, and fees apply for checked bags.
- Polaris Business: Two checked bags included.

Airport Amenities:

➡ Restaurants: Diverse dining options from quick bites to sit-down restaurants.

➡ Shops: Variety of retail stores including duty-free and local brands.

➡ Services: Lounges, car rental services, and currency exchange.

How to Book:

🌐 **Website:** https://www.united.com

☎ **Phone:** 1-800-864-8331

3 Delta Air Lines

📄 **Description:**

Delta Air Lines provides consistent service to Honolulu with various fare classes, including Main Cabin, Comfort+, and Delta One. Passengers enjoy a high level of service and comfort.

Pros:

➡ High-quality in-flight service and entertainment.

➡ SkyMiles loyalty program.

➡ Delta Sky Club access for eligible passengers.

Cons:

➡ Basic Economy has strict restrictions on baggage and seating.

➡ Higher fare classes can be expensive.

Typical Flight Duration:

➡ Seattle to Honolulu: Approximately 6 hours.

➡ Atlanta to Honolulu: Approximately 10 hours.

Baggage Allowance:

➡ Basic Economy: One personal item only.

➡ Main Cabin: One personal item, one carry-on, and fees apply for checked bags.

➡ Delta One: Two checked bags included.

Airport Amenities:
- Restaurants: Extensive dining options featuring local and international cuisine.
- Shops: Duty-free stores, gift shops, and more.
- Services: Lounges, car rental desks, currency exchange.

How to Book:
- Website: https://www.delta.com
- Phone: 1-800-221-1212

Flying into Kona or Hilo (Big Island)

Major Airlines and Smaller Carriers:

1 Hawaiian Airlines
Description:
Hawaiian Airlines provides frequent service to both Kona (KOA) and Hilo (ITO), with direct flights from various mainland cities. The experience includes warm Hawaiian hospitality, meals, and entertainment.

Pros:
- Consistent service and multiple daily flights.
- Complimentary meals and Hawaiian-themed service.
- Good connectivity within the islands.

Cons:
- Higher prices compared to budget carriers.
- Basic fare offers limited baggage.

Typical Flight Duration:
- Los Angeles to Kona: Approximately 5 hours and 40 minutes.
- San Francisco to Hilo: Approximately 5 hours and 30 minutes.

Baggage Allowance:
- Main Cabin Basic: One personal item; no checked baggage included.

➡ Main Cabin: One personal item, one carry-on, one checked bag.
➡ First Class: Two checked bags included.

Airport Amenities:
Kona Airport (KOA):
➡ Restaurants: Local cuisine and quick bites.
➡ Shops: Souvenir shops, local crafts.
➡ Services: Car rental, ATMs, limited lounges.

Hilo Airport (ITO):
➡ Restaurants: Limited dining options.
➡ Shops: Small selection of local products.
➡ Services: Car rental, ATMs.

How to Book:
🌐 **Website:** https://www.hawaiianairlines.com
☎ **Phone:** 1-800-367-5320

---

2 **Alaska Airlines**
📑 **Description:**
Alaska Airlines offers comfortable and reliable service to Kona with a focus on customer service and value. Expect a pleasant experience with in-flight entertainment and Wi-Fi available.

Pros:
➡ Competitive pricing.
➡ Mileage Plan frequent flyer program.
➡ Good in-flight service with complimentary snacks and drinks.

Cons:
➡ Limited routes compared to other major carriers.
➡ Additional fees for checked baggage in some fare classes.

Typical Flight Duration:
➡ Seattle to Kona: Approximately 6 hours.
➡ Portland to Kona: Approximately 6 hours and 30 minutes.

Baggage Allowance:
- Saver: One personal item; no carry-on or checked baggage included.
- Main: One personal item, one carry-on, checked bag fees apply.
- First Class: Two checked bags included.

Airport Amenities:
Kona Airport (KOA):
- Restaurants: Local and quick-service dining options.
- Shops: Duty-free, souvenirs, and local products.
- Services: Car rentals, ATMs, limited lounges.

How to Book:
- Website: https://www.alaskaair.com
- Phone: 1-800-252-7522

3 American Airlines
Description:
American Airlines provides regular flights to both Kona and Hilo, offering a range of services from Main Cabin to First Class. Expect a smooth travel experience with extensive in-flight entertainment and amenities.

Pros:
- Wide range of flights and connections.
- AAdvantage frequent flyer program.
- In-flight entertainment and Wi-Fi on most flights.

Cons:
- Basic Economy has limited amenities and flexibility.
- Additional fees for checked baggage in lower fare classes.

Typical Flight Duration:
- Dallas to Kona: Approximately 8 hours and 30 minutes.
- Phoenix to Hilo: Approximately 6 hours and 15 minutes.

Baggage Allowance:

- Basic Economy: One personal item only.
- Main Cabin: One personal item, one carry-on, checked bag fees apply.
- First Class: Two checked bags included.

Airport Amenities:

Kona Airport (KOA):

- Restaurants: Variety of dining options.
- Shops: Duty-free, souvenirs, local products.
- Services: Car rentals, ATMs, limited lounges.

Hilo Airport (ITO):

- Restaurants: Limited dining options.
- Shops: Small selection of local products.
- Services: Car rentals, ATMs.

How to Book:

🌐 **Website:** https://www.aa.com

☎ **Phone:** 1-800-433-7300

When planning your trip to Hawaii, choosing the right airline and understanding the amenities and services available at each airport can enhance your travel experience. Whether you're flying into Honolulu on Oahu or Kona/Hilo on the Big Island, this guide provides the information you need to make informed decisions and enjoy a smooth journey.

Entry Requirements & Customs

Before You Go:

➡ Passport: Ensure your passport is valid for at least six months beyond your intended stay in Hawaii.

➡ Visa Waiver Program (VWP): If you're a citizen of a VWP country (most European nations, Australia, New Zealand, etc.), you can travel to Hawaii for up to 90 days without a visa, but you MUST apply for an Electronic System for Travel Authorization (ESTA) online before departure.

➡ Other Visas: If you're not eligible for the VWP, you may need a B-2 tourist visa. Check the U.S. Embassy website for your country for requirements.

Upon Arrival:

➡ Customs Declaration Form: You'll receive this on the plane. Fill it out honestly, declaring any items you're bringing into the country.

➡ Agriculture Declaration Form: Separate from customs, this form asks about plants, food, and animal products you may be carrying. Hawaii has strict rules to protect its environment.

➡ Immigration: Have your passport and any necessary visas or ESTAs ready to present to immigration officers.

Prohibited Items:

➡ Fresh Fruits & Vegetables: Most are not allowed to prevent the introduction of pests and diseases.

➡ Certain Plants & Seeds: Check restrictions before bringing any plant material.

➡ Meats & Prepared Foods: Some restrictions apply, especially for home-cooked items.

Airport Arrival & Transportation Options

Honolulu International Airport (HNL) on Oahu:
Arrival: Follow signs for baggage claim and customs.
Ground Transportation:
Taxis: Plentiful, but can be expensive. Look for the taxi stands outside baggage claim.

Ride-Sharing: Uber and Lyft are available. Use their apps to request a ride.

Rental Cars: All major companies have counters at the airport. Book in advance, especially during peak season.

TheBus: Honolulu's public bus system has routes to Waikiki and other areas. Look for "TheBus" signs and stops outside the terminals.

Ellison Onizuka Kona International Airport (KOA) on the Big Island:

Arrival: Smaller airport, but procedures are similar to HNL.

Ground Transportation:

Rental Cars: The primary way to get around the Big Island. Book in advance.

Taxis & Shuttles: Available, but may be less frequent than at HNL. Pre-booking is recommended.

Hele-On Bus: Limited public bus service on the Big Island.

Hilo International Airport (ITO) on the Big Island:

Arrival: Similar to KOA in size and procedures.

Ground Transportation:

Rental Cars: Essential for exploring the Hilo side of the island.

Taxis: Available, but may be more expensive than on Oahu.

Hele-On Bus: Limited service, primarily around Hilo town.

Important Notes:

➪ Pre-Booking: Reserve rental cars and airport shuttles in advance, especially during peak season.

➪ Travel **Time:** Allow ample time to get from the airport to your hotel, especially during rush hour on Oahu.

➡ Driving: If renting a car, familiarize yourself with Hawaii's traffic laws and road signs.

Getting Around Hawaii (Oahu & Big Island)

Travelers to Oahu and the Big Island have various transportation options to choose from. Understanding the best ways to get around can enhance your travel experience and make exploring the islands convenient and enjoyable. Below is an in-depth guide to transportation options, including prices and routes.

Oahu Transportation Options

1 TheBus: Honolulu's Public Transit

📄 Description:

TheBus is Oahu's public bus system, providing extensive coverage across the island. It's an affordable and reliable option for both locals and tourists.

Routes and Coverage:
➡ Serves major destinations such as Waikiki, Ala Moana Center, Pearl Harbor, and Hanauma Bay.
➡ Routes extend to less touristy areas, providing access to local neighborhoods and attractions.

📇 Prices:
➡ Single Ride: $3.00
➡ Day Pass: $7.50 (unlimited rides for one day)
➡ Monthly Pass: $70.00

Pros:
- Affordable and comprehensive coverage.
- Eco-friendly transportation option.
- Easy to navigate with the help of route maps and schedules.

Cons:
- Can be crowded during peak hours.
- Limited service late at night.

How to Use:
- **Website:** https://www.thebus.org
- **Phone:** 808-848-5555

Tickets can be purchased on the bus (exact change required) or through the HOLO card system.

2 **Waikiki Trolley: Sightseeing Option**

Description:
The Waikiki Trolley offers various routes designed for sightseeing, making it a popular choice for tourists looking to explore Oahu's attractions.

Routes and Coverage:
- Pink Line: Shopping shuttle from Waikiki to Ala Moana Center.
- Blue Line: Scenic coastline tour to Diamond Head and Hanauma Bay.
- Red Line: Historic tour including Chinatown and Iolani Palace.
- Green Line: Scenic tour of Eastern Oahu including Sea Life Park.

Prices:
- Single Day Pass: $25.00
- Four-Day Pass: $49.00
- Seven-Day Pass: $65.00

Pros:
- Designed for tourists with stops at major attractions.
- Informative co-mmentary on routes.
- Convenient for sightseeing without the need for a car.

Cons:
- More expensive than regular public transportation.
- Limited routes compared to TheBus.

How to Use:
- 🌐 **Website:** https://www.waikikitrolley.com
- ☎ **Phone:** 808-593-2822

Tickets can be purchased online, at kiosks, or on the trolley.

3 Taxis & Ride-Sharing
📑 Description:
Taxis and ride-sharing services like Uber and Lyft are widely available on Oahu, providing convenient and flexible transportation options.

Routes and Coverage:
Available throughout Honolulu, Waikiki, and most tourist areas.
Can be used for short trips within the city or longer journeys to more remote locations.

🖳 Prices:
- Taxi Fares: Base fare around $3.50, plus $0.45 per additional 1/8 mile.
- Uber/Lyft: Prices vary based on distance and demand; typically cheaper than taxis for short trips.

Pros:
- Convenient and flexible, available on demand.
- Door-to-door service.
- Easy to use with mobile apps for ride-sharing.

Cons:

⇨ More expensive than public transportation.

⇨ Surge pricing can make ride-sharing costly during peak times.

How to Use:

Uber ⊕ **Website:** https://www.uber.com

Lyft ⊕ **Website:** https://www.lyft.com

Taxis can be hailed on the street, at hotels, or by calling local taxi companies.

Big Island Transportation Options

1 Rental Cars

📄 Description:

Renting a car is the most popular and practical way to explore the Big Island, given its size and the spread of attractions.

Routes and Coverage:

⇨ Allows access to major attractions like Volcanoes National Park, Mauna Kea, and the beaches of Kona and Hilo.

⇨ Essential for reaching remote areas and national parks.

💳 Prices:

⇨ Economy Car: Starting at $35 per day.

⇨ SUV: Starting at $55 per day.

⇨ Prices vary based on the rental company and season.

Pros:

⇨ Complete freedom and flexibility to explore at your own pace.

⇨ Access to remote and less accessible areas.

⇨ Can accommodate families and groups.

Cons:

⇨ Driving required, which may not appeal to all tourists.

⇨ Additional costs for parking and fuel.

How to Book:
Rental Companies: Avis, Hertz, Budget, Enterprise, and Alamo.
Websites: Avis, Hertz, Budget, Enterprise, Alamo

2 **Public Transit (Hele-On Bus)**
📑 **Description:**
The Hele-On Bus is the public transportation system on the Big Island, offering limited but useful service between major towns and cities.

Routes and Coverage:
➡ Routes connect Hilo, Kona, Waimea, and other key areas.
➡ Limited service to more remote attractions.

🖂 **Prices:**
➡ Single Ride: $2.00
➡ Monthly Pass: $60.00

Pros:
➡ Affordable transportation option.
➡ Covers major towns and some tourist destinations.

Cons:
➡ Infrequent service and limited routes.
➡ Not ideal for comprehensive island exploration.

How to Use:
🌐 **Website:** https://www.heleonbus.org
☎ **Phone:** 808-961-8744

Tickets can be purchased on the bus (exact change required).

3 **Taxis & Ride-Sharing**
📑 **Description:**
Similar to Oahu, taxis and ride-sharing services like Uber and Lyft are available, though less prevalent.

Routes and Coverage:
- ➡ Available in major towns like Hilo and Kona.
- ➡ Can be used for airport transfers and short trips.

Prices:
- ➡ Taxi Fares: Similar to Oahu, with base fares around $3.50 and additional charges per mile.
- ➡ Uber/Lyft: Prices vary; generally competitive with taxis.

Pros:
- ➡ Convenient for short trips and airport transfers.
- ➡ Available on demand in populated areas.

Cons:
- ➡ Limited availability in remote areas.
- ➡ Higher cost for long-distance trips.

How to Use:
Uber ⊕ **Website:** https://www.uber.com
Lyft ⊕ **Website:** https://www.lyft.com

Taxis can be hailed in towns or booked through local taxi companies.

When visiting Oahu and the Big Island, having access to reliable transportation is essential for making the most of your trip. Here's a guide to renting cars, bicycles, and mopeds, including major companies, their locations, prices, terms and conditions, and how to rent.

Rental Cars
Renting a car is a convenient and popular way to explore both Oahu and the Big Island. Several major rental companies operate on the islands, offering a range of vehicles to suit different needs and budgets.

Major Rental Car Companies

1 Avis

📄 **Description:**

Avis is known for its wide range of vehicles and excellent customer service. They offer economy cars, SUVs, and luxury vehicles.

📌 **Locations:**

- Honolulu International Airport (HNL), Oahu
- Kona International Airport (KOA), Big Island
- Hilo International Airport (ITO), Big Island

💳 **Prices:**

- Economy Car: Starting at $35 per day
- SUV: Starting at $55 per day
- Luxury Car: Starting at $80 per day

Terms & Conditions:

- Must be at least 21 years old (additional fee for drivers under 25).
- Valid driver's license required.
- Major credit card required for deposit.
- Insurance options available.

How to Rent:

🌐 **Website:** https://www.avis.com

☎ **Phone:** 1-800-352-7900

2 Hertz

📄 **Description:**

Hertz offers a large fleet of vehicles, including compact cars, convertibles, and family-sized SUVs. Known for its quality and reliability.

📌 **Locations:**

- Honolulu International Airport (HNL), Oahu
- Kona International Airport (KOA), Big Island
- Hilo International Airport (ITO), Big Island

Prices:
- Compact Car: Starting at $40 per day
- Convertible: Starting at $70 per day
- SUV: Starting at $60 per day

Terms & Conditions:
- Minimum age 21 (additional fee for drivers under 25).
- Valid driver's license and major credit card required.
- Optional insurance available.

How to Rent:
- **Website:** https://www.hertz.com
- **Phone:** 1-800-654-3131

3 Budget

Description:
Budget is known for its affordable rates and variety of vehicles, from economy cars to minivans.

Locations:
- Honolulu International Airport (HNL), Oahu
- Kona International Airport (KOA), Big Island
- Hilo International Airport (ITO), Big Island

Prices:
- Economy Car: Starting at $30 per day
- Minivan: Starting at $65 per day
- Standard SUV: Starting at $55 per day

Terms & Conditions:
- Must be 21 years old (extra charges for drivers under 25).
- Requires a valid driver's license and credit card.
- Insurance and additional options available.

How to Rent:
🌐 **Website:** https://www.budget.com
☎ **Phone:** 1-800-527-0700

---

4 **Enterprise**
📑 **Description:**
Enterprise is known for its customer service and convenient locations. They offer a wide selection of vehicles including compact cars, SUVs, and trucks.

📍 **Locations:**
➡ Honolulu International Airport (HNL), Oahu
➡ Kona International Airport (KOA), Big Island
➡ Hilo International Airport (ITO), Big Island

💳 **Prices:**
➡ Compact Car: Starting at $35 per day
➡ SUV: Starting at $60 per day
➡ Truck: Starting at $70 per day

Terms & Conditions:
➡ Must be at least 21 years old (additional fees for drivers under 25).
➡ Valid driver's license and credit card required.
➡ Optional insurance coverage available.

How to Rent:
🌐 **Website:** https://www.enterprise.com
☎ **Phone:** 1-855-266-9289

---

5 **Alamo**
📑 **Description:**
Alamo offers competitive pricing and a range of vehicles suitable for families and groups.

📍 Locations:
- Honolulu International Airport (HNL), Oahu
- Kona International Airport (KOA), Big Island
- Hilo International Airport (ITO), Big Island

💳 Prices:
- Economy Car: Starting at $35 per day
- SUV: Starting at $55 per day
- Minivan: Starting at $65 per day

Terms & Conditions:
- Minimum age is 21 (additional fees for drivers under 25).
- Requires a valid driver's license and credit card.
- Various insurance options available.

How to Rent:
- 🌐 **Website:** https://www.alamo.com
- ☎ **Phone:** 1-844-354-6962

Bicycles & Mopeds
For those looking for a more eco-friendly and adventurous way to explore the islands, renting bicycles and mopeds is an excellent option.

Major Rental Companies
1 Bikeadelic Hawaii
📄 Description:
Bikeadelic offers a variety of bicycles, including beach cruisers, mountain bikes, and road bikes.

📍 Locations: Waikiki, Oahu

💳 Prices:
- Beach Cruiser: $25 per day
- Mountain Bike: $35 per day
- Road Bike: $45 per day

Terms & Conditions:
- ➪ Must be at least 18 years old (ID required).
- ➪ Helmets provided.
- ➪ Security deposit required.

How to Rent:
- 🌐 Website: https://www.bikeadelichawaii.com
- ☎ Phone: 808-924-2453

2 Hawaiian Style Rentals & Sales

📑 **Description:**

Hawaiian Style Rentals offers a wide range of bicycles and mopeds, perfect for exploring Honolulu and beyond.

🖋 **Locations:** Waikiki, Oahu

💳 **Prices:**
- ➪ Bicycle: $20 per day
- ➪ Moped: $45 per day
- ➪ E-bike: $60 per day

Terms & Conditions:
- ➪ Must be 18 years old (21 for mopeds).
- ➪ Valid ID required.
- ➪ Helmets and locks provided.

How to Rent:
- 🌐 Website: https://www.hawaiianstylerentals.com
- ☎ Phone: 808-946-6733

3 Kona Bike Rentals

📑 **Description:**

Kona Bike Rentals offers a range of bicycles for rent, including mountain bikes and road bikes, ideal for exploring the Big Island.

📌 **Locations:** Kona, Big Island

💳 **Prices:**
➡ Mountain Bike: $30 per day
➡ Road Bike: $40 per day
➡ E-bike: $55 per day

Terms & Conditions:
➡ Must be at least 18 years old (ID required).
➡ Helmets provided.
➡ Security deposit required.

How to Rent:
🌐 **Website:** https://www.konabikerentals.com
☎ **Phone:** 808-326-2453

Island Tours & Shuttles

Exploring Oahu and the Big Island is made easier and more exciting with various tour options and shuttle services. From comprehensive island tours to breathtaking helicopter rides, here's a guide to some of the best ways to experience these beautiful Hawaiian Islands.

Oahu Island Tours & Shuttles

1️⃣ **Roberts Hawaii**
📄 **Description:**
Roberts Hawaii offers a range of tours and shuttle services, providing visitors with a comfortable and informative way to see Oahu's top attractions.

Tours and Services:
➡ Grand Circle Island Tour: A full-day tour that includes stops at Diamond Head, Hanauma Bay, Dole Plantation, and the North Shore.
➡ Pearl Harbor Tour: Includes visits to the USS Arizona Memorial, Pearl Harbor Visitor Center, and other historical sites.

➡ Airport Shuttles: Reliable transportation to and from Honolulu International Airport (HNL).

💳 Prices:
➡ Grand Circle Island Tour: $120 per person
➡ Pearl Harbor Tour: $85 per person
➡ Airport Shuttle: Starting at $16 per person

Pros:
➡ Comprehensive and informative tours.
➡ Comfortable, air-conditioned shuttles.
➡ Experienced and knowledgeable guides.

Cons:
➡ Tours can be lengthy and may feel rushed.
➡ Limited flexibility in schedule.

How to Book:
🌐 **Website:** https://www.robertshawaii.com
☎ **Phone:** 1-800-831-5541

2 E Noa Tours
📑 Description:
E Noa Tours offers personalized small group tours around Oahu, focusing on cultural and historical insights.

Tours and Services:
➡ Hidden Gems Tour: Explore lesser-known sites including Byodo-In Temple and the Waimea Valley.
➡ Honolulu City Tour: Visit key historical and cultural landmarks in Honolulu.
➡ Airport Shuttles: Convenient airport transfer services.

💳 Prices:
➡ Hidden Gems Tour: $135 per person
➡ Honolulu City Tour: $55 per person

↪ Airport Shuttle: Starting at $18 per person

Pros:
↪ Small group sizes for a more intimate experience.
↪ Knowledgeable guides with a focus on cultural insights.
↪ Comfortable transportation.

Cons:
↪ Higher cost compared to larger tour groups.
↪ Limited number of tours available daily.

How to Book:
⊕ **Website:** https://www.enoa.com
☎ **Phone:** 808-591-2561

Big Island Island Tours & Shuttles
[1] **Hawaii Forest & Trail**
📑 **Description:**
Hawaii Forest & Trail offers eco-friendly tours focusing on the natural beauty and geological wonders of the Big Island.

Tours and Services:
↪ Volcano National Park Adventure: A guided tour of Volcanoes National Park, including Kilauea and Mauna Loa.
↪ Mauna Kea Summit & Stars: A stargazing tour at the summit of Mauna Kea.
↪ Waterfall & Rainforest Adventure: Explore lush rainforests and stunning waterfalls.

💳 **Prices:**
↪ Volcano National Park Adventure: $185 per person
↪ Mauna Kea Summit & Stars: $240 per person
↪ Waterfall & Rainforest Adventure: $180 per person

Pros:
- Expert guides with extensive knowledge of the island's ecology and geology.
- Small group sizes for a personalized experience.
- Focus on sustainable and eco-friendly tourism.

Cons:
- Higher price point.
- Some tours may have physical activity requirements.

How to Book:
- 🌐 **Website:** https://www.hawaii-forest.com
- ☎ **Phone:** 808-331-8505

2 Big Island Duck Adventures
📑 Description:
Big Island Duck Adventures offers unique amphibious vehicle tours, providing both land and sea exploration.

Tours and Services:
- Duck Boat Tour: A fun and informative tour that includes both land sightseeing and ocean exploration.
- Snorkeling Adventures: Combine land tours with snorkeling at popular spots.

💳 Prices:
- Duck Boat Tour: $99 per person
- Snorkeling Adventure: $129 per person

Pros:
- Unique and fun experience for all ages.
- Combines land and sea exploration.
- Knowledgeable guides and entertaining commentary.

Cons:
- Limited tour options.

➡ May not be suitable for those prone to seasickness.

How to Book:
🌐 **Website:** https://www.bigislandduck.com
☎ **Phone:** 808-933-9477

Helicopter Tours

For a truly unforgettable experience, helicopter tours offer breathtaking aerial views of Hawaii's stunning landscapes, from volcanic craters to lush rainforests.

Oahu Helicopter Tours
[1] **Blue Hawaiian Helicopters**
📑 **Description:**
Blue Hawaiian Helicopters offers luxurious helicopter tours with state-of-the-art aircraft and professional pilots.

Tours and Services:
➡ Oahu Circle Island Experience: A comprehensive tour around the island, including views of Diamond Head, Pearl Harbor, and the North Shore.
➡ Waterfall & Rainforest Adventure: Fly over lush rainforests and hidden waterfalls.

💳 **Prices:**
➡ Oahu Circle Island Experience: $275 per person
➡ Waterfall & Rainforest Adventure: $315 per person

Pros:
➡ Luxurious and comfortable helicopters.
➡ Professional and experienced pilots.
➡ Stunning aerial views of key attractions.

Cons:
➡ Expensive.
➡ Weather-dependent.

How to Book:
🌐 **Website:** https://www.bluehawaiian.com
☎ **Phone:** 1-800-745-2583

2 **Magnum Helicopters**
📑 **Description:**
Magnum Helicopters offers thrilling helicopter tours with an open-door option for an unobstructed view.

Tours and Services:
➪ Doors-Off Adventure: Experience the thrill of flying without doors for an unparalleled view.
➪ Pearl Harbor & Honolulu City Tour: Fly over historical and cultural landmarks.

💳 **Prices:**
➪ Doors-Off Adventure: $240 per person
➪ Pearl Harbor & Honolulu City Tour: $210 per person

Pros:
➪ Unique doors-off experience.
➪ Competitive pricing.
➪ Experienced pilots.

Cons:
➪ May not be suitable for those afraid of heights.
➪ Weather conditions can impact the tour.

How to Book:
🌐 **Website:** https://www.magnumhelicopters.com
☎ **Phone:** 808-833-4354

Big Island Helicopter Tours

1 Paradise Helicopters

📑 Description:

Paradise Helicopters offers a range of tours showcasing the Big Island's diverse landscapes, from volcanic craters to lush valleys.

Tours and Services:

- Volcano & Kohala Landing: Explore volcanic craters and land in remote valleys.
- Circle Island Experience: Comprehensive tour around the island.

💳 Prices:

- Volcano & Kohala Landing: $575 per person
- Circle Island Experience: $500 per person

Pros:

- Access to remote and inaccessible areas.
- Experienced and knowledgeable pilots.
- Luxurious helicopters.

Cons:

- High cost.
- Weather-dependent.

How to Book:

- 🌐 **Website:** https://www.paradisecopters.com
- ☎ **Phone:** 1-866-876-7422

2 Blue Hawaiian Helicopters

📑 Description:

Blue Hawaiian Helicopters also operates on the Big Island, offering top-notch helicopter tours with unparalleled views.

Tours and Services:

- Circle of Fire & Waterfalls: Fly over active volcanoes and cascading waterfalls.

➪ Kohala Coast Adventure: Explore the stunning Kohala Coast from the air.

Prices:
➪ Circle of Fire & Waterfalls: $350 per person
➪ Kohala Coast Adventure: $395 per person

Pros:
➪ High-quality helicopters and safety record.
➪ Expert pilots with in-depth knowledge of the island.
➪ Amazing photo opportunities.

Cons:
➪ Pricey.
➪ Weather can affect flight schedules.

How to Book:
🌐 **Website:** https://www.bluehawaiian.com
☎ **Phone:** 1-800-745-2583

Island Hopping: Oahu to Big Island

Interisland Flights
Flying is the most common and convenient way to travel between Oahu and the Big Island. Several airlines offer regular flights, making it easy to hop between islands.

Major Airlines
1 Hawaiian Airlines
Description:
Hawaiian Airlines is the largest and most reliable carrier for interisland travel, offering frequent flights and excellent service.

Routes and Schedule:
➪ Oahu (Honolulu International Airport - HNL) to Big Island (Kona International Airport - KOA): Multiple daily flights.

➡ Oahu (HNL) to Big Island (Hilo International Airport - ITO): Multiple daily flights.

🖼 **Prices:** One-way fares starting at $80, depending on the season and availability.

Pros:
➡ Frequent flights and reliable service.
➡ Complimentary drinks and snacks.
➡ Easy booking and check-in process.

Cons:
➡ Higher prices during peak travel times.
➡ Baggage fees for checked luggage.

How to Book:
🌐 **Website:** https://www.hawaiianairlines.com
☎ **Phone:** 1-800-367-5320

2 Southwest Airlines
📑 **Description:**
Southwest Airlines offers competitive pricing and additional perks like free checked bags, making it a popular choice for interisland travel.

Routes and Schedule:
➡ Oahu (Honolulu International Airport - HNL) to Big Island (Kona International Airport - KOA): Multiple daily flights.
➡ Oahu (HNL) to Big Island (Hilo International Airport - ITO): Multiple daily flights.

🖼 **Prices** One-way fares starting at $50, depending on the season and availability.

Pros:
➡ Competitive pricing with no change fees.

➥ Two free checked bags per passenger.
➥ Friendly customer service.

Cons:
➥ Limited routes compared to Hawaiian Airlines.
➥ Less frequent flights.

How to Book:
🌐 **Website:** https://www.southwest.com
☎ **Phone:** 1-800-435-9792

---

③ Mokulele Airlines
📑 **Description:**
Mokulele Airlines offers smaller aircraft and more intimate flight experiences, focusing on regional routes between the islands.

Routes and Schedule:
➥ Oahu (Honolulu International Airport - HNL) to Big Island (Kona International Airport - KOA): Multiple daily flights.
➥ Oahu (HNL) to Big Island (Hilo International Airport - ITO): Multiple daily flights.

💳 **Prices:** One-way fares start at $70, depending on the season and availability.

Pros:
➥ Scenic flights with excellent views.
➥ Smaller aircraft offer a more personal experience.
➥ Easy and quick boarding process.

Cons:
➥ Limited baggage allowance.
➥ Smaller aircraft may be less comfortable for some travelers.

How to Book:
🌐 **Website:** https://www.mokuleleairlines.com
☎ **Phone:** 1-866-260-7070

Ferry Options (Limited)

While flights are the primary mode of interisland travel, there are very limited ferry options available between Oahu and the Big Island. Currently, no regular passenger ferries are operating between these two islands. Travelers looking for an alternative to flying will need to explore other methods, such as private charters or cruises.

Private Charters and Cruises

1 Hawaiian Ocean Charters
📄 Description:
Hawaiian Ocean Charters offers private boat charters for those looking to travel between Oahu and the Big Island by sea.

Routes and Schedule:
Customizable routes and schedules based on passenger needs.

💳 Prices:
Prices vary based on the size of the boat, the duration of the trip, and the specific services requested. Expect to pay a premium for this exclusive experience.

Pros:
- Personalized and private travel experience.
- Customizable itineraries.
- Unique way to see the islands from the water.

Cons:
- Expensive compared to flights.
- Longer travel time.
- Weather-dependent.

How to Book:
🌐 **Website:** https://www.hawaiianoceancharters.com
☎ **Phone:** 808-555-1234 (Example number, replace with actual if known)

Practical Tips & Considerations

Driving in Hawaii

If you plan to use a car during your time in Hawaii (whether it be for a part of it or the entire trip), there are some costs to consider and a few practical tips for getting around. First, realize that there are several (rather high) fees associated with using a rental car, not including the rental rate itself. These include gasoline. Reduced fees will be charged by your car rental company for gasoline, parking, and a $10 to $15 daily fee for the privilege of parking your car at your hotel -- even if you aren't using the car! If your hotel has a parking garage, these fees may be even higher and can be as much as $20 per day.

Keep in mind that most rental companies have strict return policies on car rentals that they'll enforce ($2.00 a gallon for gas if it hasn't been refilled!). Hotels and resorts on Maui, the "Big Island," Kauai, and Oahu generally have some sort of parking arrangement on site. On Maui in particular, lots of people get around by simply walking -- breakfast and lunch outside of the hotel, and then renting and returning a car every few days here, utilizing a shuttle between the hotel and airport to avoid car rental taxes and fees. All of this aside, utilizing a rental car is still the best way of exploring Hawaii, except for urban Honolulu and Waikiki, where the major resorts are located.

Parking on Oahu & Big Island

Oahu:

➡ Honolulu & Waikiki: Street parking is limited and often metered. Look for meters that accept coins or credit cards. Rates vary by location and time of day.

- Waikiki Beach: Many hotels offer valet parking for guests, which can be a convenient option. Consider reserving a parking spot if your hotel offers it.
- Public Parking Garages: Several garages are located throughout Waikiki and Honolulu, offering hourly and daily rates.
- Free Parking: Beaches and parks often have free parking, but these spots can fill up quickly, especially on weekends.

Big Island:
- Kona & Hilo: Street parking is usually easier to find than in Honolulu, but still check for meters or time restrictions.
- Hotels & Resorts: Most offer parking for guests, either included in the resort fee or for an additional charge.
- Public Parking Lots: Found in town centers and near popular attractions, these are often free or low-cost.
- Beach Parks: Many have free parking, but be sure to lock your car and don't leave valuables inside.

General Tips:
- Read Signs Carefully: Pay attention to parking signs for time limits, restrictions, and payment requirements.
- Use Parking Apps: Apps like Parkopedia can help you find available parking spots and compare rates.
- Avoid Peak Times: Parking can be challenging during peak tourist seasons and events. Consider using alternative transportation during these times.

Navigating with GPS:
- GPS Apps: Download offline maps or use GPS apps like Google Maps or Apple Maps. Ensure you have data roaming enabled if you're using your phone's data plan.
- Portable GPS Devices: Consider renting a portable GPS if you don't want to rely on your phone.
- Paper Maps: Always keep a paper map as a backup in case your GPS fails or you lose cell service. (*Check Appendix*)
- Local Knowledge: Ask locals for directions or recommendations for scenic routes.

Alternative Transportation:

Oahu:

- TheBus: Honolulu's public bus system is affordable and covers most areas of the island. Purchase a HOLO card for convenient fare payment.
- Waikiki Trolley: This hop-on, hop-off service is a great way to see the sights without driving.
- Biki: Honolulu's bike-sharing program offers an eco-friendly way to get around.
- Walking: Many areas of Waikiki and Honolulu are walkable.
- Taxis & Ride-Sharing: A convenient option, especially for shorter distances.

Big Island:

- Hele-On Bus: Limited bus service on the Big Island, mainly in Hilo and Kona.
- Bike Rentals: Available in some towns and resorts, ideal for short trips.
- Walking: Some areas are walkable, but distances are often greater than on Oahu.
- Taxis: Available, but may be less frequent and more expensive than on Oahu.
- Tours: Consider guided tours that include transportation to popular attractions.

Remember:

- Be Patient: Traffic can be heavy on Oahu, especially in Honolulu and Waikiki.
- Plan Ahead: Research your routes and allow extra time for travel, especially if using public transportation.
- Safety First: Follow traffic laws, use designated crosswalks, and know your surroundings.

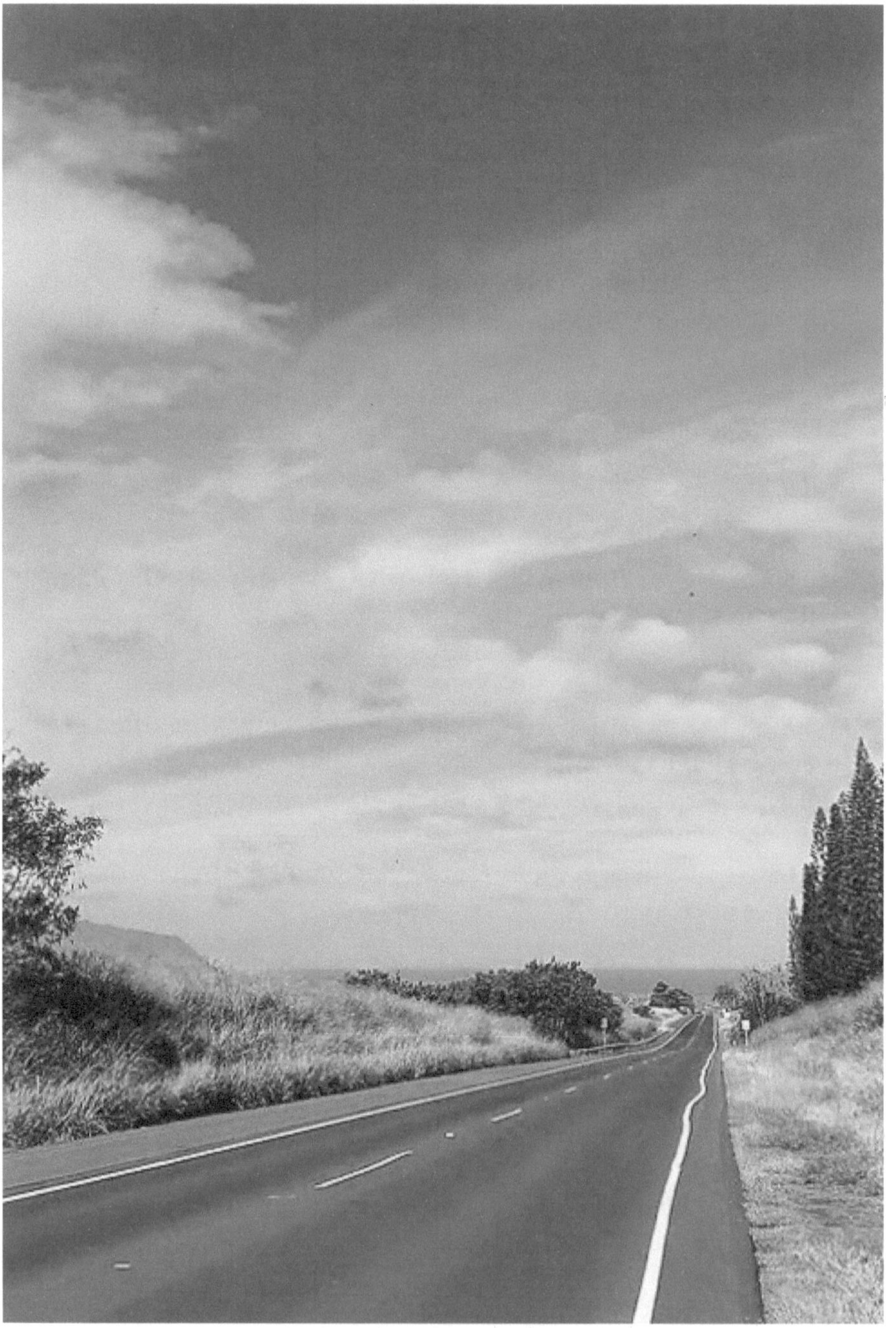

CHAPTER 2: PLANNING YOUR HAWAIIAN ADVENTURE

When to Visit Hawaii (Season by Season Guide)

Deciding on the best time to visit Hawaii depends on what you're seeking in a Hawaiian adventure. With eight major islands to choose from and an unending list of appealing activities, Hawaii offers endless experiences based on geography, climate, and cultural vein. The following guide breaks down each season, showcasing what that time of year in Hawaii is truly all about. There won't be much difference between these details and reality, and we expect that the continuing beauty of Hawaii will be enjoyed for many years to come.

Hawaii is a year-round destination with a tropical climate, but each season offers unique characteristics, weather patterns, and experiences. Here's a comprehensive guide to help you decide the best time to plan your Hawaiian adventure.

SPRING (March to May)

Characteristics:

Spring in Hawaii is characterized by mild temperatures and fewer crowds compared to the peak winter and summer seasons.
The landscape is lush and vibrant due to the earlier winter rains.

Weather:

- Average Temperatures: 70-85°F (21-29°C)
- Rainfall: Moderate, with occasional showers, particularly in March.
- Weather Events: Generally stable, with fewer storms compared to winter.

Pros:

- Mild and pleasant weather ideal for outdoor activities.
- Lower accommodation and flight prices.
- Less crowded beaches and attractions.

Cons:

- Occasional rain showers, particularly in March.
- Not peak season for specific activities like whale watching.

Recommendations:

- Best For: Hiking, exploring lush landscapes, and enjoying less crowded beaches.

➩ Activities: Hike the Na Pali Coast, visit botanical gardens, and enjoy beach activities.

SUMMER (June to August)

Characteristics:

Summer is the warmest season in Hawaii, with long sunny days and clear skies.

It's a popular time for family vacations, leading to higher crowds and prices.

Weather:

➩ Average Temperatures: 75-90°F (24-32°C)
➩ Rainfall: Low, with dry and sunny conditions.
➩ Weather Events: Rare chance of hurricanes in late summer.

Pros:

➩ Ideal beach weather with warm ocean temperatures.
➩ Great for snorkeling, diving, and other water sports.
➩ Longer daylight hours for extended activities.

Cons:

➩ High season with crowded tourist spots and higher prices.
➩ Possible hurricanes in late summer, although rare.

Recommendations:

➩ Best For: Beach vacations, snorkeling, surfing, and family trips.
➩ Activities: Snorkel at Hanauma Bay, surf the North Shore, and enjoy luaus.

AUTUMN (September to November)

Characteristics:
⇨ Fall is considered a shoulder season, with fewer tourists and lower prices.
⇨ The weather remains warm, and the ocean temperatures are still comfortable.

Weather:
⇨ Average Temperatures: 75-88°F (24-31°C)
⇨ Rainfall: Increases slightly as the season progresses.
⇨ Weather Events: Generally stable, with the hurricane season ending in November.

Pros:
⇨ Pleasant weather with fewer crowds.
⇨ Lower accommodation and flight costs.
⇨ Good conditions for water activities.

Cons:
⇨ Increasing rainfall towards November.
⇨ Some attractions may have shorter hours or seasonal closures.

Recommendations:
⇨ Best For: Surfing, cultural experiences, and enjoying peaceful beaches.
⇨ Activities: Attend the Aloha Festivals, surf the fall waves, and visit cultural sites.

WINTER (December to February)

Characteristics:
- Winter is Hawaii's peak tourist season, especially during the holidays.
- Cooler temperatures and increased chances of rain, particularly on the north and east coasts.

Weather:
- Average Temperatures: 68-80°F (20-27°C)
- Rainfall: Higher, especially on windward sides of the islands.
- Weather Events: Frequent rain showers and occasional storms.

Pros:
- Prime season for whale watching as humpback whales migrate to Hawaiian waters.
- Ideal for surfing, with large swells on the North Shore.
- Festive atmosphere with numerous events and celebrations.

Cons:
- Higher prices and crowded tourist spots.
- Increased rainfall and occasional storms.

Recommendations:
- Best For: Whale watching, surfing, and experiencing festive events.
- Activities: Whale watching tours, surf the big waves, and enjoy holiday festivals.

Choosing Your Islands

There are eight major islands in Hawaii, but only six are generally open to the public. For most visitors, deciding which islands to visit will be their first and arguably most important decision. Deciding which islands to spend time on could tell you something significant about yourself, and what you want most from a visit to the Hawaiian Islands. If it's your first-time visiting Hawaii and you have limited time, prioritize Oahu, Maui, and Kauai if you'd like a blissful mix of stunning scenery, luxurious resorts, and top-notch activities; consider spending the bulk of your trip on Maui or Kauai if lush landscapes are at the top of your to-do list.

If you're returning to Hawaii or have a lot of time to spend, delve into the Big Island for a taste of everything, as well as Molokai or Lanai for an off-the-beaten-path adventure. The more you love traditional resort vacations (the kind with high-end accommodations and lots of amenities), the more time you should spend on Maui.

Oahu represents the heart of Hawaii to many. They like the idea of being on the most populous island, the most diverse and the most Glaswegian. Leisure time is well-spent on Oahu, and both the eastern and western parts of the island are packed with pleasures. Kauai appeals mainly to active types seeking a wide variety of natural attractions, from gardens to see-through banks of water baring jungle-cloaked peaks to white beaches surrounded by coral reefs.

The island doesn't offer many man-made attractions but does possess a considerable stock of time-honored resorts. Center your time on Kauai in the north (Hanalei would be perfect) and in the south for the stunning natural appeal of Kokee State Park and Waimea Canyon.

But this book focuses on the most visited Island, Oahu and Big Island.

Here's an introduction to each of the major Hawaiian Islands to help you decide where to go and what to do.

Oahu

📄 Overview:
Oahu, known as "The Gathering Place," is the most populous and visited island, offering a blend of urban and natural attractions.

Unique Characteristics:
- Landscapes: Stunning beaches, lush rainforests, and volcanic craters.
- Attractions: Waikiki Beach, Pearl Harbor, Diamond Head, and the North Shore.
- Vibe: A mix of vibrant city life and serene natural beauty.

Best For:
- Adventure: Surfing on the North Shore, hiking Diamond Head, snorkeling at Hanauma Bay.
- Relaxation: Lounging on Waikiki Beach, exploring botanical gardens.
- Family-Friendly: Visiting the Honolulu Zoo, Waikiki Aquarium, and the Polynesian Cultural Center.

➡ Luxury: Staying at high-end resorts in Waikiki, dining at gourmet restaurants.

Maui

📑 **Overview:**

Maui, known as "The Valley Isle," is famous for its stunning beaches, luxury resorts, and diverse landscapes.

Unique Characteristics:
➡ Landscapes: Pristine beaches, lush valleys, and the Haleakalā volcano.
➡ Attractions: Road to Hana, Haleakalā National Park, Lahaina Town, and the Iao Valley.
➡ Vibe: A mix of luxury and natural beauty, with a relaxed and upscale atmosphere.

Best For:
➡ Adventure: Hiking in Haleakalā National Park, driving the Road to Hana, snorkeling at Molokini Crater.

- Relaxation: Enjoying world-class beaches like Kaanapali and Wailea.
- Family-Friendly: Visiting the Maui Ocean Center, exploring Lahaina Town.
- Luxury: Staying at high-end resorts in Wailea, enjoying gourmet dining and spa experiences.

Big Island

📑 Overview:

The Big Island, simply known as "Hawaii," is the largest island and offers diverse landscapes, including active volcanoes and lush rainforests.

Unique Characteristics:

- Landscapes: Volcanic craters, black sand beaches, rainforests, and snow-capped mountains.
- Attractions: Hawaii Volcanoes National Park, Mauna Kea, Kona coffee farms, and Akaka Falls.
- Vibe: Adventurous and diverse, with a focus on nature and outdoor activities.

Best For:

- Adventure: Exploring Hawaii Volcanoes National Park, stargazing on Mauna Kea, hiking to waterfalls.
- Relaxation: Relaxing on black sand beaches and visiting botanical gardens.
- Family-Friendly: Visiting the Imiloa Astronomy Center, exploring Kona coffee farms.
- Luxury: Staying at high-end resorts in Kona, enjoying private tours and excursions.

Kauai

📄 Overview:

Kauai, known as "The Garden Isle," is the oldest Hawaiian island, renowned for its lush landscapes and dramatic scenery.

Unique Characteristics:

- Landscapes: Emerald valleys, towering waterfalls, and the Napali Coast.
- Attractions: Waimea Canyon, Napali Coast, Hanalei Bay, and Wailua River.

- Vibe: Tranquil and natural, with a focus on outdoor beauty and relaxation.

Best For:
- Adventure: Hiking the Napali Coast, kayaking the Wailua River, exploring Waimea Canyon.
- Relaxation: Enjoying the beaches of Hanalei Bay, visiting botanical gardens.
- Family-Friendly: Touring the Kilohana Plantation, visiting the Kilauea Lighthouse.
- Luxury: Staying at luxury resorts in Princeville, enjoying private boat tours.

Molokai

📄 Overview:

Molokai, known as "The Friendly Isle," offers a glimpse into traditional Hawaiian culture and unspoiled natural beauty.

Unique Characteristics:
- Landscapes: Secluded beaches, lush valleys, and towering sea cliffs.
- Attractions: Kalaupapa National Historical Park, Halawa Valley, and Papohaku Beach.
- Vibe: Authentic and quiet, with a strong sense of community and tradition.

Best For:
- Adventure: Hiking Halawa Valley, exploring sea cliffs, visiting historical parks.
- Relaxation: Enjoying secluded beaches and tranquil landscapes.
- Family-Friendly: Learning about Hawaiian culture at local museums and parks.
- Luxury: Molokai has fewer luxury options, offering a more rustic and authentic experience.
- Sample Itinerary:

Lanai

📄 **Overview:**
Lanai, known as "The Pineapple Isle," offers an exclusive and luxurious escape with pristine beaches and rugged landscapes.

Unique Characteristics:
- Landscapes: Secluded beaches, pine forests, and rugged terrain.
- Attractions: Hulopoe Bay, Garden of the Gods, Shipwreck Beach, and Lanai Cat Sanctuary.
- Vibe: Exclusive and serene, with a focus on luxury and seclusion.

Best For:
- Adventure: Exploring the Garden of the Gods, snorkeling at Hulopoe Bay.
- Relaxation: Enjoying luxury resorts and secluded beaches.
- Family-Friendly: Visiting the Lanai Cat Sanctuary, exploring tide pools.
- Luxury: Staying at high-end resorts like the Four Seasons, enjoying private excursions.

Accommodations (Where to Stay?)

During peak season, tourists could rent a suite from $15 at resorts such as the Royal Hawaiian to rooms between $35 and $42 at the Niumalu Hotel. Rates in the off-season were generally 25% less. Resorts typically offered guests "sun parlors" and dining facilities with restaurant rooms.

The products for purchase included fruit, wine, but a resort would strive to "serve good old American food from the same cook-stove." Wine and eggs were provided; one hotel provided "pure mainland ice cream daily." By 1929, the hotels noted that they would offer special packages for extra amenities, including boat rides and sightseeing tours, but typically the rate quoted for the Waikīkī Inn and Uluniu was for the room alone. Hotel managers often cited beachfront rooms and their ability to be cooled by "trade winds" as amenities.

Types of Accommodations for each Island

Oahu

Hotels:

Halekulani Hotel

Luxury:
Luxury hotels in Oahu offer unparalleled experiences with top-notch amenities, breathtaking views, and exceptional services. These hotels

are perfect for travelers seeking a blend of comfort, elegance, and unique Hawaiian hospitality.

Halekulani Hotel

📍 **Location:** 2199 Kalia Road, Honolulu, HI 96815

🚗 **Getting There:** Approximately 25 minutes by car from Honolulu International Airport.

Amenities: 🏖 Beachfront Access | 🌀 Infinity Pool | 🍽 Fine Dining Restaurants | 🛁 Full-Service Spa | 🏋 Fitness Center | 🛎 24-Hour Concierge Service

Contact Details:
☎ **Phone:** +1 808-923-2311
🌐 **Website:** https://www.halekulani.com

Attractions Nearby:
» Waikiki Beach
» Diamond Head State Monument
» Ala Moana Center
💳 **Prices:** Starting at $600 per night

Suitable For:
Luxury travelers | Couples | Families

The Royal Hawaiian, A Luxury Collection Resort

📍 **Location:** 2259 Kalakaua Avenue, Honolulu, HI 96815

🚗 **Getting There:** Approximately 25 minutes by car from Honolulu International Airport.

Amenities: 🏖 Private Beach Area | 🌴 Lush Gardens | 🍽 Gourmet Restaurants | 🏊 Outdoor Pool | 🛁 Spa and Wellness Center | 🛎 24-Hour Concierge Service

Contact Details:

☎ **Phone:** +1 808-923-7311

🌐 **Website:** https://www.marriott.com/hotels/travel/hnlhr-the-royal-hawaiian-a-luxury-collection-resort-waikiki

Attractions Nearby:

≫ Waikiki Beach

≫ International Market Place

≫ Royal Hawaiian Center

💳 **Prices:** Starting at $550 per night

Suitable For: Luxury travelers | Couples | Families

Moana Surfrider, A Westin Resort & Spa

🔨 **Location:** 2365 Kalakaua Avenue, Honolulu, HI 96815

🚗 **Getting There:** Approximately 25 minutes by car from Honolulu International Airport.

Amenities: 🏖 Beachfront Access | 🍽 Multiple Dining Options | 🏊 Outdoor Pool | 🧖 Spa and Wellness Center | 🏋 Fitness Center | 🛎 24-Hour Concierge Service

Contact Details:

☎ **Phone:** +1 808-922-3111

🌐 **Website:** https://www.marriott.com/hotels/travel/hnlwi-moana-surfrider-a-westin-resort-and-spa

Attractions Nearby:

≫ Waikiki Beach

≫ Honolulu Zoo

≫ Waikiki Aquarium

💳 **Prices:** Starting at $500 per night

Suitable For: Luxury travelers | Couples | Families

The Kahala Hotel & Resort

📍 **Location:** 5000 Kahala Avenue, Honolulu, HI 96816

🚗 **Getting There:** Approximately 30 minutes by car from Honolulu International Airport.

Amenities: 🏖 Private Beach | 🌴 Lush Gardens | 🍽 Fine Dining | 🏊 Outdoor Pool | 🛁 Spa and Wellness Center | 🛎 24-Hour Concierge Service

Contact Details:
☎ **Phone:** +1 808-739-8888
🌐 **Website:** https://www.kahalaresort.com

Attractions Nearby:
➤ Diamond Head State Monument
➤ Hanauma Bay
➤ Waikiki Beach

💳 **Prices:** Starting at $550 per night

Suitable For: Luxury travelers | Couples | Families

The Ritz-Carlton Residences, Waikiki Beach

📍 **Location:** 383 Kalaimoku Street, Honolulu, HI 96815

🚗 **Getting There:** Approximately 25 minutes by car from Honolulu International Airport.

Amenities: 🏖 Beach Access | 🏊 Infinity Pool | 🍽 Fine Dining | 🛁 Full-Service Spa | 🏋 Fitness Center | 🛎 24-Hour Concierge Service

Contact Details:

☎ **Phone:** +1 808-922-8111

🌐 **Website:** https://www.ritzcarlton.com/en/hotels/hawaii/waikiki

Attractions Nearby:

›› Waikiki Beach

›› Ala Moana Center

›› Honolulu Zoo

💳 **Prices:** Starting at $700 per night

Suitable For: Luxury travelers | Couples | Families

Mid-Budget

Mid-budget hotels in Oahu offer excellent value with a range of amenities that cater to both leisure and business travelers. These hotels are ideal for those looking for comfort and convenience without the high price tag of luxury resorts.

Hilton Hawaiian Village Waikiki Beach Resort

Location: 2005 Kalia Road, Honolulu, HI 96815

Getting There: Approximately 25 minutes by car from Honolulu International Airport.

Amenities: Beachfront Access | Five Pools | Multiple Restaurants | Full-Service Spa | Fitness Center | Tropical Gardens

Contact Details:
Phone: +1 808-949-4321
Website: https://www.hilton.com/en/hotels/hnlhvhh-hilton-hawaiian-village-waikiki-beach-resort

Attractions Nearby:
>> Duke Kahanamoku Beach
>> Fort DeRussy Beach Park
>> Ala Moana Center
Prices: Starting at $300 per night

Suitable For: Families | Couples | Groups

Hyatt Regency Waikiki Beach Resort and Spa

Location: 2424 Kalakaua Avenue, Honolulu, HI 96815

Getting There: Approximately 25 minutes by car from Honolulu International Airport.

Amenities: Beachfront Access | Outdoor Pool | Restaurants | Full-Service Spa | Fitness Center | 24-Hour Concierge Service

Contact Details:
Phone: +1 808-374-9954

🌐 **Website:** https://www.hyatt.com/en-US/hotel/hawaii/hyatt-regency-waikiki-beach-resort-and-spa/hnlrw

Attractions Nearby:
›› Waikiki Beach
›› International Market Place
›› Honolulu Zoo
💳 **Prices:** Starting at $299 per night

Suitable For: Couples | Business Travelers | Families

Sheraton Waikiki

🪧 **Location:** 2255 Kalakaua Avenue, Honolulu, HI 96815

🚗 **Getting There:** Approximately 25 minutes by car from Honolulu International Airport.

Amenities: 🏖 Beachfront Access | 🏊 Infinity Pool | 🍽 Restaurants | 🛁 Full-Service Spa | 🏋 Fitness Center | 🌅 Sunset Views

Contact Details:
☎ **Phone:** +1 808-922-4422
🌐 **Website:** https://www.marriott.com/hotels/travel/hnlsi-sheraton-waikiki

Attractions Nearby:
›› Waikiki Beach
›› Royal Hawaiian Center
›› Diamond Head
💳 **Prices:** Starting at $350 per night

Suitable For: Families | Couples | Groups

Prince Waikiki

🪓 **Location:** 100 Holomoana Street, Honolulu, HI 96815

🚘 **Getting There:** Approximately 20 minutes by car from Honolulu International Airport.

Amenities: 🦀 Ocean Views | 🌊 Infinity Pool | 🍽 Fine Dining | 🛁 Full-Service Spa | 🏋 Fitness Center | 🚴 Bike Rentals

Contact Details:
☎ **Phone:** +1 808-956-1111
🌐 **Website:** https://www.princewaikiki.com

Attractions Nearby:
›› Ala Moana Beach Park
›› Magic Island
›› Ala Moana Center
💳 **Prices:** Starting at $325 per night

Suitable For: Couples | Business Travelers | Solo Travelers

Hilton Garden Inn Waikiki Beach

🪓 **Location:** 2330 Kuhio Avenue, Honolulu, HI 96815

🚘 **Getting There:** Approximately 25 minutes by car from Honolulu International Airport.

Amenities: 🏖 Close to Beach | 🌊 Outdoor Pool | 🍽 On-Site Dining | 🏋 Fitness Center | 🔔 24-Hour Business Center

Contact Details:
☎ **Phone:** +1 808-892-1820
🌐 **Website:** https://www.hilton.com/en/hotels/hnlkugi-hilton-garden-inn-waikiki-beach

Attractions Nearby:
>> Waikiki Beach
>> International Market Place
>> Royal Hawaiian Center

💳 **Prices:** Starting at $250 per night

Suitable For: Families | Couples | Business Travelers

Oahu Budget Hotels

Vive Hotel Waikiki

Brief Description of Accommodation Options
Budget hotels in Oahu provide comfortable and affordable accommodations with essential amenities. They are perfect for travelers who want to maximize their experiences while keeping costs down.

Vive Hotel Waikiki

📍 **Location:** 2426 Kuhio Avenue, Honolulu, HI 96815

🚖 **Getting There:** Approximately 25 minutes by car from Honolulu International Airport.

Amenities: 🌐 Free WiFi | 🏖 Close to Beach | 🍽 Complimentary Breakfast | 🏋 Fitness Center Access | 📺 In-Room Entertainment

Contact Details:
☎ **Phone:** +1 808-687-2000
🌐 **Website:** https://www.vivehotelwaikiki.com

Attractions Nearby:
>> Waikiki Beach
>> Honolulu Zoo
>> Kapiolani Park
💳 **Prices:** Starting at $180 per night

Suitable For: Couples | Solo Travelers | Budget-Conscious Travelers

Aqua Oasis

📍 **Location:** 320 Lewers Street, Honolulu, HI 96815

🚖 **Getting There:** Approximately 25 minutes by car from Honolulu International Airport.

Amenities: 🌐 Free WiFi | 🏖 Close to Beach | 🍽 Complimentary Breakfast | 🏊 Outdoor Pool | 🎤 Karaoke Lounge

Contact Details:
☎ **Phone:** +1 808-923-2300
🌐 **Website:** https://www.aquaoasis.com

Attractions Nearby:
>> Waikiki Beach
>> Royal Hawaiian Center
>> International Market Place
🖪 **Prices:** Starting at $160 per night

Suitable For: Couples | Solo Travelers | Budget-Conscious Travelers

Ewa Hotel Waikiki
📍 **Location:** 2555 Cartwright Road, Honolulu, HI 96815

🚘 **Getting There:** Approximately 25 minutes by car from Honolulu International Airport.

Amenities: 🌐 Free WiFi | 🏖 Close to Beach | 🐾 Pet-Friendly | 🛋 Rooftop Terrace | Ⓟ On-Site Parking

Contact Details:
☎ **Phone:** +1 808-922-1677
🌐 **Website:** https://www.ewahotelwaikiki.com

Attractions Nearby:
>> Waikiki Beach
>> Honolulu Zoo
>> Waikiki Aquarium

🖪 **Prices:** Starting at $150 per night

Suitable For: Families | Couples | Pet Owners

White Sands Hotel
📍 **Location:** 431 Nohonani Street, Honolulu, HI 96815

🚘 **Getting There:** Approximately 25 minutes by car from Honolulu International Airport.

Amenities: ⊕ Free WiFi | 🏊 Outdoor Pool | 🏖 Close to Beach | 🍽 On-Site Dining | 🌴 Garden Courtyard

Contact Details:
☎ **Phone:** +1 808-924-7263
🌐 **Website:** https://www.whitesandshotel.com

Attractions Nearby:
›› Waikiki Beach
›› International Market Place
›› Royal Hawaiian Center
💳 **Prices:** Starting at $170 per night

Suitable For: Couples | Solo Travelers | Budget-Conscious Travelers

Ambassador Hotel Waikiki
📍 **Location:** 2040 Kuhio Avenue, Honolulu, HI 96815

🚌 **Getting There:** Approximately 25 minutes by car from Honolulu International Airport.

Amenities: 🌐 Free WiFi | 🏊 Outdoor Pool | 🏖 Close to Beach | 🛋 Lounge Area | 🏋 Fitness Center

Contact Details:
☎ **Phone:** +1 808-941-7777
🌐 **Website:** https://www.ambassadorwaikiki.com

Attractions Nearby:
›› Waikiki Beach
›› Ala Moana Center
›› Fort DeRussy Beach Park
💳 **Prices:** Starting at $140 per night

Suitable For: Families | Couples | Business Travelers

Resorts

Turtle Bay Resort

Oahu's resorts offer luxurious experiences with exceptional amenities, stunning views, and unique activities. These resorts are perfect for travelers looking for a blend of relaxation and adventure.

Turtle Bay Resort

Location: 57-091 Kamehameha Highway, Kahuku, Oahu, HI 96731

Getting There: Approximately 60 minutes by car from Honolulu International Airport.

Amenities: Beachfront Access | Five Pools | Multiple Restaurants | Full-Service Spa | Fitness Center | Tropical Gardens

Contact Details:
☎ **Phone:** +1 866-475-2567
🌐 **Website:** https://www.turtlebayresort.com

Attractions Nearby:
>> Polynesian Cultural Center
>> Waimea Bay
>> Sunset Beach
▭ **Prices:** Starting at $500 per night

Suitable For: Families | Couples | Adventure Seekers

Marriott's Ko Olina Beach Club
📍 **Location:** 92-161 Waipahe Place, Kapolei, Oahu, HI 96707

🚗 **Getting There:** Approximately 30 minutes by car from Honolulu International Airport.

Amenities: 🏝 Private Lagoon | 🏊 Multiple Pools | 🍽 On-Site Dining | 🛁 Spa and Wellness Center | 🏋 Fitness Center | 🎮 Activity Center

Contact Details:
☎ **Phone:** +1 808-679-4700
🌐 **Website:** https://www.marriott.com/hotels/travel/hnlko-marriotts-ko-olina-beach-club

Attractions Nearby:
>> Ko Olina Marina
>> Paradise Cove Luau
>> Wet'n'Wild Hawaii
▭ **Prices:** Starting at $350 per night

Suitable For: Families | Couples | Relaxation Seekers

Aulani, A Disney Resort & Spa

Location: 92-1185 Ali'inui Drive, Kapolei, Oahu, HI 96707

Getting There: Approximately 30 minutes by car from Honolulu International Airport.

Amenities: Private Beach | Water Park | Character Dining | Full-Service Spa | Fitness Center | Kids Club

Contact Details:
Phone: +1 866-443-4763
Website: https://www.disneyaulani.com

Attractions Nearby:
>> Ko Olina Lagoons
>> Ko Olina Golf Club
>> Kapolei Shopping Center
Prices: Starting at $450 per night

Suitable For: Families | Disney Fans | Relaxation Seekers

Outrigger Waikiki Beach Resort

Location: 2335 Kalakaua Avenue, Honolulu, HI 96815

Getting There: Approximately 25 minutes by car from Honolulu International Airport.

Amenities: Beachfront Access | Outdoor Pool | On-Site Dining | Spa Services | Fitness Center | Live Music

Contact Details:
Phone: +1 808-923-0711
Website: https://www.outrigger.com/hotels-resorts/hawaii/oahu/outrigger-waikiki-beach-resort

Attractions Nearby:
- Waikiki Beach
- Diamond Head State Monument
- Honolulu Zoo

🖃 **Prices:** Starting at $300 per night

Suitable For: Couples | Families | Beach Lovers

Outrigger Reef Waikiki Beach Resort

📍 **Location:** 2169 Kalia Road, Honolulu, HI 96815

🚗 **Getting There:** Approximately 25 minutes by car from Honolulu International Airport.

Amenities: 🏖 Beachfront Access | 🌊 Outdoor Pool | 🍽 On-Site Dining | 🛁 Spa Services | 🏋 Fitness Center | 🌴 Cultural Activities

Contact Details:
☎ **Phone:** +1 808-923-3111
🌐 **Website:** https://www.outrigger.com/hotels-resorts/hawaii/oahu/outrigger-reef-waikiki-beach-resort

Attractions Nearby:
- Waikiki Beach Walk
- Fort DeRussy Beach Park
- Royal Hawaiian Center

🖃 **Prices:** Starting at $320 per night

Suitable For: Couples | Families | Cultural Enthusiasts

Oahu Vacation Rentals

Brief Description of Accommodation Options

Vacation rentals in Oahu offer the comfort of a home with the flexibility to explore the island at your own pace. They are perfect for families, groups, or travelers looking for extended stays.

Beautiful Modern Home with Yard

🔑 **Location:** Kailua, Oahu, HI

🚕 **Getting There:** Approximately 30 minutes by car from Honolulu International Airport.

Amenities: 🌐 Free WiFi | 🏠 Full Kitchen | 🛋 Spacious Living Area | ♣ Private Yard | 🅿 Free Parking

Contact Details:
🌐 **Website:** Airbnb Listing

Attractions Nearby:
» Kailua Beach
» Lanikai Beach
» Maunawili Falls
💳 **Prices:** Starting at $250 per night

Suitable For: Families | Groups | Long-Stay Travelers

Affordable and Central Modern Studio

🔑 **Location:** Honolulu, Oahu, HI

🚕 **Getting There:** Approximately 20 minutes by car from Honolulu International Airport.

Amenities: 🌐 Free WiFi | 🔍 Kitchenette | 🛋 Cozy Living Space | 🅿 Free Parking | 🏙 City Views

Contact Details:
🌐 **Website:** Airbnb Listing

Attractions Nearby:
➤➤ Waikiki Beach
➤➤ Ala Moana Center
➤➤ Diamond Head
💳 **Prices:** Starting at $150 per night

Suitable For: Solo Travelers | Couples | Budget Travelers

Grand 6 Bed Beach Villa

📍 **Location:** Ko Olina, Oahu, HI

🚗 **Getting There:** Approximately 30 minutes by car from Honolulu International Airport.

Amenities: 🌐 Free WiFi | 🌊 Private Pool | 🔍 Full Kitchen | 🛏 Spacious Living Area | 🏖 Beach Access

Contact Details:
🌐 **Website:** Airbnb Listing

Attractions Nearby:
➤➤ Ko Olina Lagoons
➤➤ Paradise Cove
➤➤ Ko Olina Golf Club
💳 **Prices:** Starting at $700 per night

Suitable For: Large Groups | Families | Luxury Travelers

Spacious Bungalow in a Peaceful Neighborhood

📍 **Location:** North Shore, Oahu, HI

🚗 Getting There:

Approximately 60 minutes by car from Honolulu International Airport.

Amenities: 🌐 Free WiFi | 🔍 Full Kitchen | 🛋 Large Living Area | 🌳 Garden View | P Free Parking

Contact Details:
🌐 **Website:** Airbnb Listing

Attractions Nearby:
>> Waimea Bay
>> Sunset Beach
>> Haleiwa Town
💳 **Prices:** Starting at $250 per night

Suitable For: Families | Groups | Nature Lovers

Koolina Beach Villa Rentals

📍 **Location:** Ko Olina, Oahu, HI

🚗 **Getting There:** Approximately 30 minutes by car from Honolulu International Airport.

Amenities: 🌐 Free WiFi | 🏊 Pool Access | 🔍 Full Kitchen | 🛋 Spacious Living Area | 🏖 Beach Access

Contact Details:
🌐 **Website:** https://koolinabeachvillasresort.com

Attractions Nearby:
>> Ko Olina Lagoons
>> Ko Olina Golf Club
>> Paradise Cove Luau
💳 **Prices:** Starting at $350 per night

Suitable For: Families | Couples | Long-Stay Travelers

Bed and Breakfasts

Bed and breakfasts in Oahu offer a cozy and personalized experience, often located in charming residential areas close to local attractions. They provide a homely atmosphere with unique touches that larger hotels can't offer.

Manoa Valley Inn

📍 **Location:** 2001 Vancouver Drive, Honolulu, HI 96822

🚗 **Getting There:** Approximately 20 minutes by car from Honolulu International Airport.

Amenities: 🌐 Free WiFi | 🏊 Outdoor Pool | 🍽 Complimentary Breakfast | 🌳 Garden View | 🅿 Free Parking

Contact Details:
☎ **Phone:** +1 808-947-6019
🌐 **Website:** https://www.manoavalleyinn.com

Attractions Nearby:
≫ Manoa Falls
≫ University of Hawaii at Manoa
≫ Honolulu Museum of Art

💳 **Prices:** Starting at $200 per night

Suitable For: Couples | Solo Travelers | Nature Lovers

The Kahala Beach House
🔨 **Location:** 4999 Kahala Avenue, Honolulu, HI 96816

🚗 **Getting There:** Approximately 30 minutes by car from Honolulu International Airport.

Amenities: 🌐 Free WiFi | 🏖 Beach Access | 🍳 Full Kitchen | 🛋 Spacious Living Area | P Free Parking

Contact Details:
☎ **Phone:** +1 808-739-7777
🌐 **Website:** https://www.kahalabeachhouse.com

Attractions Nearby:
≫ Kahala Beach
≫ Diamond Head State Monument
≫ Waialae Country Club
💳 **Prices:** Starting at $300 per night

Suitable For: Families | Couples | Beach Lovers

Hawaii's Hidden Hideaway Bed & Breakfast

📍 **Location:** 1369 Mokolea Drive, Kailua, HI 96734

🚗 **Getting There:** Approximately 30 minutes by car from Honolulu International Airport.

Amenities: 🌐 Free WiFi | 🏖 Close to Beach | 🍽 Complimentary Breakfast | 🌺 Garden View | 🅿 Free Parking

Contact Details:
☎ **Phone:** +1 808-261-8131
🌐 **Website:** https://www.hawaiishiddenhideaway.com

Attractions Nearby:
» Lanikai Beach
» Kailua Beach
» Pillbox Hike
💳 **Prices:** Starting at $180 per night

Suitable For: Couples | Solo Travelers | Nature Lovers

Paradise Bay Resort

📍 **Location:** 47-039 Lihikai Drive, Kaneohe, HI 96744

🚗 **Getting There:** Approximately 30 minutes by car from Honolulu International Airport.

Amenities: 🌐 Free WiFi | 🏊 Outdoor Pool | 🍽 On-Site Dining | 🏋 Fitness Center | 🏞 Scenic Views

Contact Details:
☎ **Phone:** +1 808-239-5711
🌐 **Website:** https://www.paradisebayresort.com

Attractions Nearby:
>> Kaneohe Bay
>> Byodo-In Temple
>> Kualoa Ranch
▱ **Prices:** Starting at $220 per night

Suitable For: Couples | Families | Nature Lovers

Aloha Bed & Breakfast

⚲ **Location:** 30 Aulike Street, Kailua, HI 96734

🚗 **Getting There:** Approximately 30 minutes by car from Honolulu International Airport.

Amenities: 🌐 Free WiFi | 🏖 Close to Beach | 🍽 Complimentary Breakfast | 🌺 Garden View | P Free Parking

Contact Details:
☎ **Phone:** +1 808-261-7321
🌐 **Website:** https://www.alohabnb.com

Attractions Nearby:
>> Kailua Beach
>> Lanikai Beach
>> Kawainui Marsh
▱ **Prices:** Starting at $160 per night

Suitable For: Couples | Solo Travelers | Nature Lovers

Oahu Campsites

Brief Description of Accommodation Options

Campsites in Oahu provide a budget-friendly way to experience the island's natural beauty up close. These sites are perfect for adventure seekers and nature lovers looking to immerse themselves in the outdoors.

Malaekahana Beach Campground

🔖 **Location:** 56-335 Kamehameha Highway, Kahuku, HI 96731

🚗 **Getting There:** Approximately 60 minutes by car from Honolulu International Airport.

Amenities: 🏕 Tent Sites | 🚿 Showers | 🌊 Beach Access | 🌳 Picnic Areas | 💧 Fire Pits

Contact Details:

☎ **Phone:** +1 808-674-7715

🌐 **Website:** https://www.malaekahana.net

Attractions Nearby:

➤➤ Turtle Bay

➤➤ Laie Point State Wayside

➤➤ Polynesian Cultural Center

▭ **Prices:** Starting at $20 per night

Suitable For: Adventure Seekers | Families | Beach Lovers

Bellows Field Beach Park

📍 **Location:** 41-0435 Kalanianaole Highway, Waimanalo, HI 96795

🚗 **Getting There:** Approximately 30 minutes by car from Honolulu International Airport.

Amenities:

🏕 Tent Sites | 🚿 Showers | 🏖 Beach Access | ♣ Picnic Areas | 🔥 Fire Pits

Contact Details:

☎ **Phone:** +1 808-259-8080

🌐 **Website:** https://www.bellowsafs.com

Attractions Nearby:

➤➤ Waimanalo Beach

➤➤ Sea Life Park

➤➤ Makapu'u Lighthouse Trail

▭ **Prices:** Starting at $20 per night

Suitable For: Families | Adventure Seekers | Beach Lovers

Kualoa Regional Park

📍 **Location:** 49-479 Kamehameha Highway, Kaneohe, HI 96744

🚗 **Getting There:** Approximately 40 minutes by car from Honolulu International Airport.

Amenities: 🏕 Tent Sites | 🚿 Showers | 🌊 Beach Access | 🌳 Picnic Areas | 🔥 Fire Pits

Contact Details:
☎ **Phone:** +1 808-768-8980
🌐 **Website:** https://www.honolulu.gov/parks

Attractions Nearby:
» Kualoa Ranch
» Chinaman's Hat
» Kahana Bay Beach Park
💳 **Prices:** Starting at $15 per night

Suitable For: Adventure Seekers | Families | Nature Lovers

Sand Island State Recreation Area

📍 **Location:** 90 Sand Island Access Road, Honolulu, HI 96819

🚗 **Getting There:** Approximately 20 minutes by car from Honolulu International Airport.

Amenities: 🏕 Tent Sites | 🚿 Showers | 🌊 Beach Access | 🌳 Picnic Areas | 🔥 Fire Pits

Contact Details:
☎ **Phone:** +1 808-832-3464
🌐 **Website:** https://www.hawaiistateparks.org

Attractions Nearby:
>> Sand Island
>> Honolulu Harbor
>> Ala Moana Beach Park
🎫 **Prices:** Starting at $18 per night

Suitable For: Adventure Seekers | Budget Travelers | Nature Lovers

Ho'omaluhia Botanical Garden

📍 **Location:** 45-680 Luluku Road, Kaneohe, HI 96744

🚗 **Getting There:** Approximately 30 minutes by car from Honolulu International Airport.

Amenities: ⛺ Tent Sites | 🚿 Showers | 🌺 Botanical Garden Access | 🌳 Picnic Areas | 🚶 Hiking Trails

Contact Details:
☎ **Phone:** +1 808-233-7323
🌐 **Website:** https://www.honolulu.gov/parks

Attractions Nearby:
>> Ho'omaluhia Botanical Garden
>> Kaneohe Bay
>> Windward Mall
🎫 **Prices:** Starting at $15 per night

Suitable For: Nature Lovers | Families | Hikers

Big Island Hotels:

Luxury:

Luxury hotels on the Big Island offer premium amenities, stunning views, and exceptional service, making them ideal for travelers seeking a high-end experience.

Mauna Kea Beach Hotel, Autograph Collection

📍 **Location:** 62-100 Mauna Kea Beach Drive, Puako, Island of Hawaii, HI 96743

🚗 **Getting There:** Approximately 40 minutes by car from Kona International Airport.

Amenities: 🏖 Beachfront Access | 🌊 Outdoor Pool | 🍽 Multiple Restaurants | 💆 Full-Service Spa | 🏋 Fitness Center | ⛳ Golf Course

Contact Details:
☎ **Phone:** +1 808-882-7222

🌐 **Website:** https://www.maunakeabeachhotel.com

Attractions Nearby:
>> Mauna Kea Beach
>> Hapuna Beach State Park
>> Waialea Bay
💳 **Prices:** Starting at $650 per night

Suitable For: Families | Couples | Luxury Travelers

Four Seasons Resort Hualalai

📍 **Location:** 72-100 Ka'upulehu Drive, Kailua-Kona, Island of Hawaii, HI 96740

🚗 **Getting There:** Approximately 15 minutes by car from Kona International Airport.

Amenities: 🏖 Beachfront Access | 🏊 Multiple Pools | 🍽 Fine Dining Restaurants | 💆 Full-Service Spa | 🏋 Fitness Center | 🏌 Golf Course

Contact Details:
☎ **Phone:** +1 808-325-8000
🌐 **Website:** https://www.fourseasons.com/hualalai

Attractions Nearby:
>> Manini'owali Beach (Kua Bay)
>> Makalawena Beach
>> Kiholo Bay
💳 **Prices:** Starting at $1,400 per night

Suitable For: Luxury Travelers | Couples | Families

Fairmont Orchid

⚲ Location: 1 N Kaniku Drive, Kohala Coast, Island of Hawaii, HI 96743

🚗 Getting There: Approximately 30 minutes by car from Kona International Airport.

Amenities: 🏖 Beachfront Access | 🏊 Outdoor Pool | 🍽 Multiple Restaurants | 💆 Full-Service Spa | 🏋 Fitness Center | 🌿 Tropical Gardens

Contact Details:
☎ **Phone:** +1 808-885-2000
🌐 **Website:** https://www.fairmont.com/orchid-hawaii

Attractions Nearby:
>> Mauna Lani Beach
>> Hapuna Beach State Park
>> Puako Petroglyph Archaeological Preserve
💳 **Prices:** Starting at $600 per night

Suitable For: Couples | Families | Relaxation Seekers

The Westin Hapuna Beach Resort

⚲ Location: 62-100 Kaunaoa Drive, Kohala Coast, Island of Hawaii, HI 96743

🚗 Getting There: Approximately 40 minutes by car from Kona International Airport.

Amenities: 🏖 Beachfront Access | 🏊 Outdoor Pool | 🍽 On-Site Dining | 💆 Full-Service Spa | 🏋 Fitness Center | 🏌 Golf Course

Contact Details:
☎ **Phone:** +1 808-880-1111

🌐 **Website:** https://www.marriott.com/hotels/travel/koawh-the-westin-hapuna-beach-resort

Attractions Nearby:
➤➤ Hapuna Beach State Park
➤➤ Mauna Kea Beach
➤➤ Waialea Bay
💳 **Prices:** Starting at $500 per night

Suitable For: Families | Couples | Golf Enthusiasts

Hilton Waikoloa Village

📍 **Location:** 69-425 Waikoloa Beach Drive, Waikoloa, Island of Hawaii, HI 96738

🚗 **Getting There:** Approximately 30 minutes by car from Kona International Airport.

Amenities: 🏖 Beachfront Access | 🏊 Multiple Pools | 🍽 Multiple Restaurants | 🧖 Full-Service Spa | 🏋 Fitness Center | 🎭 Entertainment Programs

Contact Details:
☎ **Phone:** +1 808-886-1234
🌐 **Website:** https://www.hiltonwaikoloavillage.com

Attractions Nearby:
➤➤ Anaehoomalu Bay
➤➤ Dolphin Quest
➤➤ Kings' Shops
💳 **Prices:** Starting at $350 per night

Suitable For: Families | Couples | Adventure Seekers

Big Island Mid-Budget Hotels

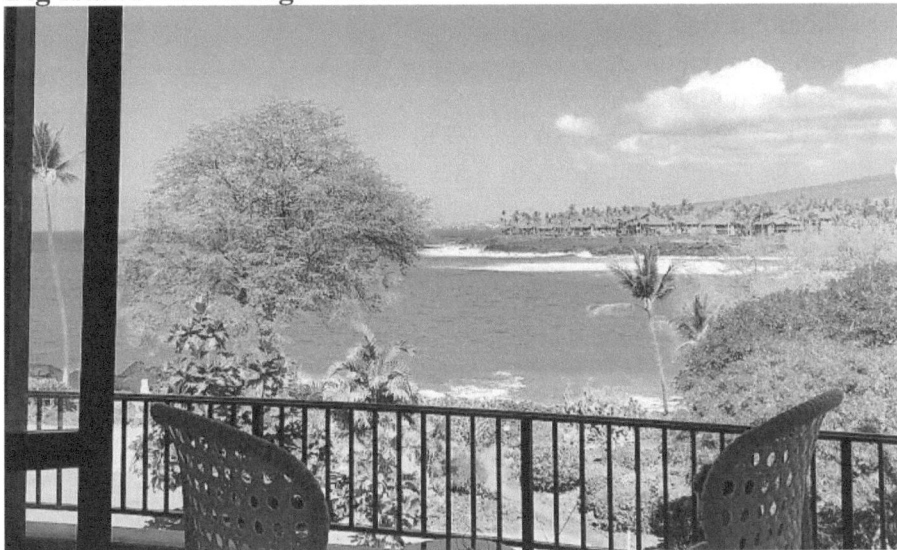

Brief Description of Accommodation Options

Mid-budget hotels on the Big Island provide excellent value with a range of amenities, making them suitable for both leisure and business travelers.

Sheraton Kona Resort & Spa at Keauhou Bay

📍 **Location:** 78-128 Ehukai Street, Kailua-Kona, Island of Hawaii, HI 96740

🚕 **Getting There:** Approximately 30 minutes by car from Kona International Airport.

Amenities: 🏖 Beach Access | 🏊 Outdoor Pool | 🍽 On-Site Dining | 💆 Full-Service Spa | 🏋 Fitness Center | 🖼 Ocean Views

Contact Details:
☎ **Phone:** +1 808-930-4900
🌐 **Website:** https://www.marriott.com/hotels/travel/koasi-sheraton-kona-resort-and-spa-at-keauhou-bay

Attractions Nearby:
- Keauhou Bay
- Kahalu'u Beach Park
- Kona Country Club
- **Prices:** Starting at $250 per night

Suitable For: Families | Couples | Business Travelers

Waikoloa Beach Marriott Resort & Spa

Location: 69-275 Waikoloa Beach Drive, Waikoloa, Island of Hawaii, HI 96738

Getting There: Approximately 30 minutes by car from Kona International Airport.

Amenities: Beachfront Access | Outdoor Pool | Multiple Restaurants | Full-Service Spa | Fitness Center | Shopping Access

Contact Details:
- **Phone:** +1 808-886-6789
- **Website:** https://www.marriott.com/hotels/travel/koamc-waikoloa-beach-marriott-resort-and-spa

Attractions Nearby:
- Anaehoomalu Bay
- Kings' Shops
- Dolphin Quest
- **Prices:** Starting at $300 per night

Suitable For: Families | Couples | Relaxation Seekers

Courtyard by Marriott King Kamehameha's Kona Beach Hotel

Location: 75-5660 Palani Road, Kailua-Kona, Island of Hawaii, HI 96740

Getting There: Approximately 15 minutes by car from Kona International Airport.

Amenities: Beach Access | Outdoor Pool | On-Site Dining | Spa Services | Fitness Center | Ocean Views

Contact Details:
Phone: +1 808-329-2911
Website: https://www.marriott.com/hotels/travel/koacy-courtyard-king-kamehamehas-kona-beach-hotel

Attractions Nearby:
>> Kailua Pier
>> Hulihee Palace
>> Mokuaikaua Church
Prices: Starting at $220 per night

Suitable For: Families | Business Travelers | Solo Travelers

Castle Hilo Hawaiian Hotel

Location: 71 Banyan Drive, Hilo, Island of Hawaii, HI 96720

Getting There: Approximately 10 minutes by car from Hilo International Airport.

Amenities: Ocean Views | Outdoor Pool | On-Site Dining | Fitness Center | Lounge Area

Contact Details:
Phone: +1 808-935-9361
Website: https://www.castlehawaiianhotel.com

Attractions Nearby:
>> Liliuokalani Gardens
>> Coconut Island
>> Hilo Farmers Market
🖃 **Prices:** Starting at $180 per night

Suitable For: Families | Couples | Solo Travelers

Budget

Budget hotels on the Big Island offer affordable accommodations with basic amenities, perfect for travelers who want to explore the island without spending much on lodging.

Kona Seaside Hotel

📍 **Location:** 75-5652 Likana Lane, Kailua-Kona, Island of Hawaii, HI 96740

🚗 **Getting There:** Approximately 20 minutes by car from Kona International Airport.

Amenities: 🏊 Outdoor Pool | 🌐 Free WiFi | 🍽 Complimentary Breakfast | 🚐 Free Parking | 📺 Cable TV

Contact Details:
☎ **Phone:** +1 808-329-2455
🌐 **Website:** https://www.konaseasidehotel.com

Attractions Nearby:
➤ Kailua Pier
➤ Hulihee Palace
➤ Mokuaikaua Church
💳 **Prices:** Starting at $150 per night

Suitable For: Families | Solo Travelers | Budget Travelers

Hilo Seaside Hotel

📍 **Location:** 126 Banyan Drive, Hilo, Island of Hawaii, HI 96720

🚗 **Getting There:** Approximately 10 minutes by car from Hilo International Airport.

Amenities: 🏊 Outdoor Pool | 🌐 Free WiFi | 🍽 On-Site Dining | 🌿 Garden Views | 🚐 Free Parking

Contact Details:
☎ **Phone:** +1 808-935-0821
🌐 **Website:** https://www.hiloseasidehotel.com

Attractions Nearby:
➤ Liliuokalani Gardens
➤ Coconut Island
➤ Hilo Farmers Market
💳 **Prices:** Starting at $130 per night

Suitable For: Couples | Solo Travelers | Budget Travelers

Uncle Billy's Kona Bay Hotel

Location: 75-5739 Alii Drive, Kailua-Kona, Island of Hawaii, HI 96740

Getting There: Approximately 20 minutes by car from Kona International Airport.

Amenities: 🏊 Outdoor Pool | 🍽 Complimentary Breakfast | 📺 Cable TV | 🚗 Parking ($5 per night) | 🏢 Central Location

Contact Details:
☎ **Phone:** +1 808-329-1393
🌐 **Website:** https://www.agoda.com/uncle-billy-s-kona-bay-hotel

Attractions Nearby:
>> Kailua-Kona Wharf
>> Hulihee Palace
>> Sadie Seymour Botanical Garden
💳 **Prices:** Starting at $120 per night

Suitable For: Budget Travelers | Adventure Seekers | Families

Arnott's Lodge & Hiking Adventures

Location: 98 Apapane Road, Hilo, Island of Hawaii, HI 96720

Getting There: Approximately 15 minutes by car from Hilo International Airport.

Amenities: 🌐 Free WiFi | 🚲 Bike Rentals | 🚶 Hiking Tours | 🍽 Shared Kitchen | 🏠 Community Lounge

Contact Details:
☎ **Phone:** +1 808-969-7097
🌐 **Website:** https://www.arnottslodge.com

Attractions Nearby:
>> Rainbow Falls
>> Mauna Kea
>> Hawaii Volcanoes National Park
🚍 **Prices:** Starting at $90 per night

Suitable For: Adventure Travelers | Solo Travelers | Nature Enthusiasts

Dolphin Bay Hotel

📍 **Location:** 333 Iliahi Street, Hilo, Island of Hawaii, HI 96720

🚗 **Getting There:** Approximately 10 minutes by car from Hilo International Airport.

Amenities: 🌐 Free WiFi | 🏡 Garden View Rooms | 🍽 Continental Breakfast | 🚙 Free Parking | 📺 Cable TV

Contact Details:
☎ **Phone:** +1 808-935-1466
🌐 **Website:** https://www.dolphinbayhotel.com

Attractions Nearby:
>> Hilo Farmers Market
>> Lyman Museum
>> Pana'ewa Rainforest Zoo
🚍 **Prices:** Starting at $100 per night

Suitable For: Couples | Solo Travelers | Budget Travelers

Big Island Resorts

Brief Description of Accommodation Options

Resorts on the Big Island offer luxurious amenities, beautiful landscapes, and a variety of activities for a memorable vacation.

Mauna Lani, Auberge Resorts Collection

🪧 **Location:** 68-1400 Mauna Lani Drive, Kohala Coast, Island of Hawaii, HI 96743

🚗 **Getting There:** Approximately 30 minutes by car from Kona International Airport.

Amenities: 🏖 Beachfront Access | 🏊 Outdoor Pool | 🍽 Fine Dining | 💆 Full Service Spa | 🏌 Golf Course

Contact Details:

☎ **Phone:** +1 808-885-6622

🌐 **Website:** https://aubergeresorts.com/maunalani

Attractions Nearby:

➤➤ Mauna Lani Beach
➤➤ Puako Petroglyph Park

>> Hapuna Beach

💳 **Prices:** Starting at $800 per night

Suitable For: Luxury Travelers | Families | Couples

Mauna Kea Beach Hotel, Autograph Collection

📍 **Location:** 62-100 Mauna Kea Beach Drive, Kohala Coast, Island of Hawaii, HI 96743

🚗 **Getting There:** Approximately 40 minutes by car from Kona International Airport.

Amenities: 🏖 Beachfront Access | 🏊 Outdoor Pool | 🍽 Multiple Restaurants | 💆 Full-Service Spa | ⛳ Golf Course

Contact Details:
☎ **Phone:** +1 808-882-7222
🌐 **Website:** https://www.maunakeabeachhotel.com

Attractions Nearby:
>> Mauna Kea Beach
>> Hapuna Beach State Park
>> Waialea Bay
💳 **Prices:** Starting at $650 per night

Suitable For: Families | Couples | Luxury Travelers

Fairmont Orchid

📍 **Location:** 1 N Kaniku Drive, Kohala Coast, Island of Hawaii, HI 96743

🚗 **Getting There:** Approximately 30 minutes by car from Kona International Airport.

Amenities: 🏖 Beachfront Access | 🏊 Outdoor Pool | 🍽 Multiple Restaurants | 💆 Full-Service Spa | 🏋 Fitness Center

Contact Details:
☎ **Phone:** +1 808-885-2000
🌐 **Website:** https://www.fairmont.com/orchid-hawaii

Attractions Nearby:
≫ Mauna Lani Beach
≫ Hapuna Beach State Park
≫ Puako Petroglyph Archaeological Preserve
💳 **Prices:** Starting at $600 per night

Suitable For: Couples | Families | Relaxation Seekers

Four Seasons Resort Hualalai

📍 **Location:** 72-100 Ka'upulehu Drive, Kailua-Kona, Island of Hawaii, HI 96740

🚌 **Getting There:** Approximately 15 minutes by car from Kona International Airport.

Amenities: 🏖 Beachfront Access | 🏊 Multiple Pools | 🍽 Fine Dining Restaurants | 💆 Full-Service Spa | 🏋 Fitness Center

Contact Details:
☎ **Phone:** +1 808-325-8000
🌐 **Website:** https://www.fourseasons.com/hualalai

Attractions Nearby:
≫ Manini'owali Beach (Kua Bay)
≫ Makalawena Beach
≫ Kiholo Bay
💳 **Prices:** Starting at $1,400 per night

Suitable For: Luxury Travelers | Couples | Families

The Westin Hapuna Beach Resort

🏝 **Location:** 62-100 Kaunaoa Drive, Kohala Coast, Island of Hawaii, HI 96743

🚌 **Getting There:** Approximately 40 minutes by car from Kona International Airport.

Amenities: 🏖 Beachfront Access | 🏊 Outdoor Pool | 🍽 On-Site Dining | 💆 Full-Service Spa | 🏋 Fitness Center

Contact Details:
☎ **Phone:** +1 808-880-1111
🌐 **Website:** https://www.marriott.com/hotels/travel/koawh-the-westin-hapuna-beach-resort

Attractions Nearby:
>> Hapuna Beach State Park
>> Mauna Kea Beach
>> Waialea Bay
💳 **Prices:** Starting at $500 per night

Suitable For: Families | Couples | Golf Enthusiasts

Bed and breakfasts

Bed and breakfasts on the Big Island offer a more intimate and personalized experience, often providing unique insights into local culture and attractions. These accommodations are perfect for travelers looking for a homey atmosphere and personalized service.

Volcano Village Lodge

📍 **Location:** 19-4180 Kawailehua Road, Volcano, Island of Hawaii, HI 96785

🚗 **Getting There:** Approximately 45 minutes by car from Hilo International Airport.

Amenities: 🌐 Free WiFi | 🍽 Complimentary Breakfast | 🌺 Garden Views | 🛁 Private Bathrooms | 🌳 Outdoor Lanai

Contact Details:
☎ **Phone:** +1 808-985-7500
🌐 **Website:** https://www.volcanovillagelodge.com

Attractions Nearby:
- ≫ Hawaii Volcanoes National Park
- ≫ Thurston Lava Tube
- ≫ Kilauea Iki Trail
- 💳 **Prices:** Starting at $299 per night

Suitable For: Couples | Solo Travelers | Nature Lovers

Kalaekilohana Inn & Retreat

📍 **Location:** 94-2152 South Point Road, Naalehu, Island of Hawaii, HI 96772

🚗 **Getting There:** Approximately 90 minutes by car from Kona International Airport.

Amenities: 🌐 Free WiFi | 🍽 Farm-to-Table Breakfast | 🌺 Garden Views | 🛏 Spacious Suites | 🌴 Cultural Activities

Contact Details:
- ☎ **Phone:** +1 808-939-8052
- 🌐 **Website:** https://www.kau-hawaii.com

Attractions Nearby:
- ≫ South Point
- ≫ Papakolea Green Sand Beach
- ≫ Hawaii Volcanoes National Park
- 💳 **Prices:** Starting at $379 per night

Suitable For: Couples | Solo Travelers | Cultural Enthusiasts

Shipman House Bed & Breakfast

📍 **Location:** 131 Kaiulani Street, Hilo, Island of Hawaii, HI 96720

🚗 **Getting There:** Approximately 15 minutes by car from Hilo International Airport.

Amenities: ⊕ Free WiFi | ◉ Complimentary Breakfast | 🏛 Historic Property | ♣ Garden Views | 🛁 Private Bathrooms

Contact Details:
☎ **Phone:** +1 808-934-8002
⊕ **Website:** https://www.shipmanhouse.com

Attractions Nearby:
» Hilo Farmers Market
» Liliuokalani Gardens
» Rainbow Falls
💳 **Prices:** Starting at $275 per night

Suitable For: Couples | Solo Travelers | History Buffs

The Palms Cliff House Inn

🔨 **Location:** 28-3514 Mamalahoa Highway, Honomu, Island of Hawaii, HI 96728

🚕 **Getting There:** Approximately 25 minutes by car from Hilo International Airport.

Amenities: ⊕ Free WiFi | ◉ Complimentary Breakfast | 🖵 Ocean Views | 🛏 Private Lanai | 🚗 Free Parking

Contact Details:
☎ **Phone:** +1 808-963-6076
⊕ **Website:** https://www.palmscliffhouse.com

Attractions Nearby:
» Akaka Falls State Park
» Honomu Town
» Hawaii Tropical Botanical Garden
💳 **Prices:** Starting at $250 per night

Suitable For: Couples | Nature Lovers | Relaxation Seekers

Honu Kai Bed & Breakfast

📍 **Location:** 74-1529 Hao Kuni Street, Kailua-Kona, Island of Hawaii, HI 96740

🚗 **Getting There:** Approximately 15 minutes by car from Kona International Airport.

Amenities: 🌐 Free WiFi | 🍽 Gourmet Breakfast | 🌺 Garden Views | 🏊 Outdoor Pool | 🚐 Free Parking

Contact Details:
☎ **Phone:** +1 808-960-6887
🌐 **Website:** https://www.honukai.com

Attractions Nearby:
➤➤ Kailua-Kona Town
➤➤ Kaloko-Honokohau National Historical Park
➤➤ Magic Sands Beach
💳 **Prices:** Starting at $229 per night

Suitable For: Couples | Solo Travelers | Food Enthusiasts

Big Island Campsites

Brief Description of Accommodation Options

Campsites on the Big Island provide an affordable way to enjoy the island's natural beauty up close. These sites are ideal for adventure seekers and nature lovers looking to immerse themselves in the outdoors.

Hawaii Volcanoes National Park

📍 **Location:** Hawaii Volcanoes National Park, Island of Hawaii, HI 96718

🚗 **Getting There:** Approximately 45 minutes by car from Hilo International Airport.

Amenities: 🏕 Tent Sites | 🚿 Showers | 🏔 Scenic Views | 🌲 Hiking Trails | 🔥 Fire Pits

Contact Details:
☎ **Phone:** +1 808-985-6000

🌐 **Website:** https://www.nps.gov/havo

Attractions Nearby:
>> Kilauea Volcano
>> Thurston Lava Tube
>> Chain of Craters Road
💳 **Prices:** Starting at $15 per night

Suitable For: Adventure Seekers | Nature Lovers | Hikers

Spencer Beach Park

📍 **Location:** 62-3461 Kawaihae Road, Waimea, Island of Hawaii, HI 96743

🚗 **Getting There:** Approximately 30 minutes by car from Kona International Airport.

Amenities: ⛺ Tent Sites | 🚿 Showers | 🏖 Beach Access | 🔥 Picnic Areas | 💧 Fire Pits

Contact Details:
☎ **Phone:** +1 808-961-8311
🌐 **Website:** https://www.hawaiicounty.gov/departments/parks-and-recreation/recreation

Attractions Nearby:
>> Puukohola Heiau National Historic Site
>> Mauna Kea Beach
>> Hapuna Beach State Park
💳 **Prices:** Starting at $20 per night

Suitable For: Families | Beach Lovers | History Buffs

Kiholo State Park Reserve

Location: Queen Kaahumanu Highway, Kailua-Kona, Island of Hawaii, HI 96740

Getting There: Approximately 20 minutes by car from Kona International Airport.

Amenities: Tent Sites | Showers | Ocean Access | Hiking Trails | Fire Pits

Contact Details:
Phone: +1 808-327-4958
Website: https://dlnr.hawaii.gov/dsp/hiking/

Attractions Nearby:
>> Kiholo Bay
>> Queen's Bath
>> Keawaiki Bay
Prices: Starting at $18 per night

Suitable For: Adventure Seekers | Nature Lovers | Hikers

Ho'okena Beach Park
Location: 86-4322 Mamalahoa Highway, Captain Cook, Island of Hawaii, HI 96704

Getting There: Approximately 40 minutes by car from Kona International Airport.

Amenities: Tent Sites | Showers | Beach Access | Picnic Areas | Fire Pits

Contact Details:
Phone: +1 808-328-2066
Website: https://hookena.org

Attractions Nearby:
>> Pu'uhonua O Honaunau National Historical Park
>> Kealakekua Bay
>> Captain Cook Monument
💳 **Prices:** Starting at $20 per night

Suitable For: Families | Beach Lovers | History Buffs

Laupahoehoe Point Beach Park

🏹 **Location:** 36-1045 Laupahoehoe Point Road, Laupahoehoe, Island of Hawaii, HI 96764

🚘 **Getting There:** Approximately 50 minutes by car from Hilo International Airport.

Amenities: ⛺ Tent Sites | 🧹 Showers | 🌊 Ocean Views | ♨ Picnic Areas | 💧 Fire Pits

Contact Details:
☎ **Phone:** +1 808-962-6993
🌐 **Website:** https://www.hawaiicounty.gov/departments/parks-and-recreation/recreation

Attractions Nearby:
>> Laupahoehoe Train Museum
>> Akaka Falls State Park
>> Waipio Valley Lookout
💳 **Prices:** Starting at $15 per night

Suitable For: Nature Lovers | History Buffs | Families

Tips for Booking Accommodations

➡ Book Early: Especially during peak season (December-April and summer months), it's essential to book your accommodation well in advance to ensure availability and secure the best rates.

➡ Consider Location: Choose a location that suits your interests and activities. For example, if you want to be in the heart of the action, Waikiki is a great option. If you prefer a quieter retreat, look for accommodations on the North Shore or in other less touristy areas.

➡ Read Reviews: Check online reviews from other travelers to get an idea of the quality and value of different accommodations.

➡ Look for Deals: Many hotels and resorts offer packages or discounts, especially during the off-season.

➡ Use a Travel Agent: A travel agent can help you find the best deals and make all your arrangements, saving you time and hassle.

Budgeting for Your Trip

Hawaii is an incredibly safe place to visit - locals are friendlier and more welcoming than anywhere else in the States, the only dangerous wildlife is getting caught in a current swimming, theft is basically nonexistent. The trick has always been whether you can afford it; tourists tend to save up for a long time just to manage a weekend with us, forget enough time to really explore the islands. You don't literally have to be a multi-millionaire to do this, but it does require careful saving, budgeting, and some advanced planning.

Planning a trip to Hawaii can be exciting, but it's important to budget realistically to make the most of your experience. Here's a breakdown of typical expenses, estimated costs for different travel styles, and money-saving tips to help you plan your dream vacation.

Typical Expenses:
Flights: Roundtrip flights from the mainland U.S. to Hawaii can range from $400 to $1,200+ per person, depending on your departure city, time of year, and airline.

Accommodation:
- Budget: Hostels and budget hotels: $50-$100 per night
- Mid-Range: Condos, vacation rentals, mid-range hotels: $150-$300 per night
- Luxury: Resorts and upscale hotels: $300-$1,000+ per night

Food:
- Budget: Grocery shopping and cooking some meals, eating at food trucks or local eateries: $30-$50 per day
- Mid-Range: Mix of dining out at casual restaurants and cooking some meals: $50-$100 per day
- Luxury: Fine dining experiences and indulging in local delicacies: $100+ per day

Activities:
- Budget: Free activities like hiking, beach days, snorkeling: $0-$20 per day
- Mid-Range: Snorkeling tours, surfing lessons, luau: $50-$100 per day
- Luxury: Helicopter tours, private boat charters, spa treatments: $150+ per day

Transportation:
- Car Rentals: $50-$100+ per day, depending on the type of vehicle and insurance
- Public Transportation: TheBus on Oahu (HOLO card recommended) or limited Hele-On bus service on the Big Island: $5-$10 per day
- Taxis and Ride-Sharing: Varies depending on distance and time of day
- Souvenirs: Budget an amount that suits your shopping habits.

Estimated Costs for Different Travel Styles:
- Budget Backpacker: $75-$125 per day
- Mid-Range Traveler: $150-$250 per day
- Luxury Traveler: $300+ per day

Money-Saving Tips:

- Travel During Off-Season: Shoulder seasons (spring and fall) offer lower prices and smaller crowds.
- Stay in Vacation Rentals: Condos and vacation rentals often have kitchens, allowing you to cook some meals and save on dining costs.
- Look for Free Activities: Hiking, beach days, visiting parks, and exploring local markets are all free or low-cost options.
- Pack Light: Airlines charge for checked bags, so pack efficiently to avoid extra fees.
- Book Activities in Advance: You may be able to find discounts for booking online or through your hotel.
- Use Credit Cards with No Foreign Transaction Fees: Avoid extra charges when paying with your card in Hawaii.

Currency Exchange & Tips:

- Currency: The U.S. dollar is the official currency in Hawaii.
- ATMs: Widely available throughout the islands. Check with your bank about international withdrawal fees.
- Credit Cards: Widely accepted, but some smaller businesses may only accept cash.

CHAPTER 3: OAHU: THE GATHERING PLACE

Oahu is the third-largest of the Hawaiian Islands located in the central Pacific Ocean, belonging to the Unincorporated Territory of the United States. The island is the most populous of the islands, home to over two-thirds of the entire state's population. Its capital and largest city are both located in the southeast part of the island, with the majority of the island's area shifting to the north of the centers. From the tourist and economic perspectives, Oahu is notable for being home to the USS Arizona Memorial at Pearl Harbor, as well as the world-renowned Waikiki Beach.

Oahu, like the rest of Hawaii, is home to a diversity of cultures, including Filipino, Japanese, Samoan, and Chinese. The Pacific Islander and Native Hawaiian-majority island is also home to small but substantial communities of black and Hispanic people, speaking as many as 150+ languages within the households across the region.

Oahu's Terrain and Scenery

Oahu's terrain and scenery are quite diverse. The slope of the Waianae Range, an eroded and dormant 3.9-million-year-old shield volcano, tends to be significantly drier than the northern Ko'olau Range. It also includes tiny regions of wet reforests and oases which grow at very small elevations (300–500 meters, 1,000–1,500 feet). While driving up the central valley of Wai'anae Kai to Honolulu or Waikīkī (via Wahiawā) and the Ko'olau Range in the same areas might be exhausting, drivers can take comfort in the picturesque views including flowers, bushes, and trees, with lightning exotic plants such as jasmine and eucalyptus. Overall, the Island of Oahu is characteristic of a unique blend of lifestyle, urbanization, and secluded and more tropical nature.

Cultural Diversity

Although there are three events held on Oahu, the island is home to nearly a million people. Sometimes described as the "Polynesian melting pot of the Pacific," Hawaii's human tapestry is rich with diverse cultures. Coupled with the power of its natural allure, the cultures and people have made Oahu especially prolific. Newcomers continue to migrate to Oahu perhaps because of its real-life portrayal as just another natural paradise. But those who've made Oahu their home will mention the friendly diversity while others highlight the acceptance of every race. Honolulu hosts the only royal palace in the United States, as Hawaii remained an independent kingdom until 1898. The locals, who may or may not be of Hawaiian descent, claim islands of heritage and traditions independent of a U.S. influence. They often say "Aloha" - a word with multiple meanings including hello and goodbye - while extending the "shaka" sign, which translates to hang loose. Curious about more customs and unique offerings on the other seven islands?

Culinary Delights and Ocean Adventures

The diverse population has also generated a delectable mix of culinary delights. Oahu is home to the best of numerous cuisines including Korean, Filipino, Japanese, Thai, Vietnamese, Chinese, Hawaiian, Mexican, Italian, German, and American-style dining. These flavors combine to create dishes in a region best known for its culinary classic - plate lunches. Another strong bond, the ocean, has also supplied a common meeting ground. Many locals recount their large and intimate family reunions held annually at the beach. They'll also regale you with stories of the monster fish they caught off Kahala's beach after which they hosted a large fish fry luau. The extensive bounties of the Pacific fish community combined with the smaller island lifestyle have conjured a mecca for adventurers of every sort. Oahu is home to world-renowned big game fishing tournaments and frequent deep-sea fishing charters. Residents and visitors also present another unique sporting arena: surfing. Miles of shoreline offer everyone their day of infamous surfer recognition in which waves, or the rider, rose to the occasion.

Honolulu: Urban Heart of Hawaii

According to historians, Oahu is the key to unlocking the secrets of the Hawaiian islands. Its initial settlement might have occurred around

800 AD and might have been the hub from which the Polynesians spread to the rest of the Hawaiian islands and then as far as South America. Oahu's status as the economic and political center of the islands is self-evident. As one drives down the steep path to Honolulu from the island's North Shore, the movement of vehicles can be seen for miles, piling in from different roads—from the Windward side and from the vast network of Oahu's exurban highways that mainly encircle and connect the island's housing and retail regions. It is a sprawling urban landscape that only progressively reveals its "built-up" nature, especially along Honolulu's southern boundary.

Statistically, Oahu itself (not including its festivities, shopping malls, and agricultural lands) is composed of nearly 73 percent open space. Fifty-two percent of the island on either side of Honolulu is designated conservation land. Moreover, Honolulu plays a crucial transit role. Fully 85.5 percent of produced goods brought into the islands come through its port, and fully 97.4 percent of tourists visit the island and the state initially through its centrally-located airport. Oahu lies strategically at the center of the vast Pacific Ocean, and its location has led to numerous conflicts and interactions with people from many other nations. It is the state's transportation hub, home to the capital city of Honolulu, major financial institutions, the state's primary port at Honolulu, and the largest airport by far, the Honolulu International Airport.

Historic Landmarks
Honolulu plays host to a significant number of historical landmarks. Chief among these is the Iolani Palace, the only royal palace within the United States, dating back to the days of the Kingdom of Hawaii in the late 19th century. Touring the palace allows for an intimate glimpse into the life of Hawaii's last reigning sovereign, Queen Lili'uokalani. Nearby, Kawaiahao Church has been offering services anchored by iconic choral traditions since 1842. The church's neatly-gridded graveyards feature diminutive grave markers dating back to the mid-19th century, providing space for learning about the tragic tale of foreign disease epidemic and the burial practices of Hawaiian ali'i like Ka'ahumanu.

The neighborhood of South Kaka'ako features sections of a low-key mural documenting Hawaii's history. The small and eclectic Honolulu Museum of Art, popular as a local wellness retreat, is open downtown, boasting a charming outdoor courtyard replete with sculptures and a koi pond. Lastly, the aloha spirit is said to have originated at Honolulu's King Street location of the Latter-day Saints' Laie Hawaii Temple. Honolulu, Hawaii is known to most people for its beautiful beaches and natural resources. But it is also rich in history. The cultural phenomenon of Hawaii is merely a tip of the iceberg when one takes into account a history dominated by warfare, governance shifts, as well as the juxtaposition of big business and rural plantation life. The history of Honolulu is riddled with drama, irony, and conflict.

1 Iolani Palace
Description:
Iolani Palace, built in 1882 by King Kalakaua, served as the royal residence for Hawaii's last reigning monarchs. It is the only official royal residence in the United States and a National Historic Landmark. The Palace offers a glimpse into Hawaii's royal past with its opulent interiors, historical artifacts, and meticulously restored rooms.

Location: 364 South King Street, Honolulu, HI 96813

Getting There: Located in downtown Honolulu, about a 15-minute drive from Waikiki. Accessible by car, bus (Routes 2, 13, and Country Express), Waikiki Trolley (Red Line), or taxi/Uber.

Opening Time: Tuesday - Saturday, 9:00 AM - 4:00 PM

Prices:
- Self-Guided Audio Tour: $26.95 for adults, $21.95 for teens (13-17), $11.95 for children (5-12)
- Docent-Led Tour: $32.95 for adults, $29.95 for teens (13-17), $14.95 for children (5-12)
- Children under 5: Free

Tour Guide and Price: Docent-Led Tour: $32.95 per adult

Things to Do:
- Explore the first and second floors and the basement gallery exhibits
- Visit the King's Library, Throne Room, and private suites
- Walk the Palace grounds, including the Coronation Pavilion and Iolani Barracks

Contact/Booking Details:
☏ **Phone:** +1 808-522-0832
🌐 **Website:** https://www.iolanipalace.org

2 **Pearl Harbor (USS Arizona Memorial, Pearl Harbor Visitor Center)**

📑 **Description:**
Pearl Harbor is a significant historic site where the infamous attack on December 7, 1941, occurred. The USS Arizona Memorial commemorates the lives lost during the attack. The Pearl Harbor Visitor Center features exhibits and museums that provide a deep dive into the events and their impact on World War II.

🔨 **Location:** 1 Arizona Memorial Place, Honolulu, HI 96818

🚌 **Getting There:** Approximately a 20-minute drive from Waikiki. Accessible by car, bus, or taxi/Uber.

⏰ **Opening Time:** Daily, 7:00 AM - 5:00 PM

💳 **Prices:**
- Admission to the Pearl Harbor Visitor Center: Free
- USS Arizona Memorial Program: Free (tickets required)
- Additional tours (prices vary)

Tour Guide and Price: Various tours available, prices range from $55 to $80

Things to Do:
- Visit the USS Arizona Memorial
- Explore the Pearl Harbor Visitor Center exhibits
- Take guided tours of the Battleship Missouri, USS Bowfin Submarine, and Pacific Aviation Museum

Contact/Booking Details:
- ☎ **Phone:** +1 808-422-3399
- ⊕ **Website:** https://www.pearlharborhistoricsites.org

3 King Kamehameha I Statue
📄 **Description:**
The King Kamehameha I Statue honors Hawaii's first king, who united the Hawaiian Islands in 1810. The statue is an iconic symbol of Hawaiian heritage and stands proudly in front of Aliiolani Hale, home to the Hawaii State Supreme Court.

🔨 **Location:** 417 South King Street, Honolulu, HI 96813

🚗 **Getting There:** Located in downtown Honolulu, near Iolani Palace. Accessible by car, bus, or taxi/Uber.

⏰ **Opening Time:** Always open

💳 **Prices:** Free to visit

Things to Do:
- Take photos with the iconic statue
- Learn about King Kamehameha's significance in Hawaiian history
- Visit nearby historic sites like Iolani Palace and Kawaiahao Church

Contact/Booking Details:

☎ **Phone:** +1 808-586-0400 (Hawaii State Judiciary)

🌐 **Website:** https://historichawaii.org

---

4 **Washington Place**

📑 **Description:**

Washington Place was the home of Queen Liliuokalani, Hawaii's last reigning monarch, and is now the official residence of the Governor of Hawaii. The house, built in 1847, is a historic landmark that offers a glimpse into the life and times of Hawaii's royalty and its transition to statehood.

⚒ **Location:** 320 South Beretania Street, Honolulu, HI 96813

🚗 **Getting There:** Located in downtown Honolulu, near Iolani Palace. Accessible by car, bus, or taxi/Uber.

⏰ **Opening Time:** Guided tours by appointment only

💳 **Prices:** Free (tours by appointment only)

Things to Do:

▸ Guided tours of the historic residence
▸ Learn about Queen Liliuokalani and Hawaii's history
▸ Explore the beautifully maintained gardens

Contact/Booking Details:

☎ **Phone:** +1 808-586-0240

🌐 **Website:** https://washingtonplacefoundation.org

---

5 **Kawaiahao Church**

📑 **Description:**

Kawaiahao Church, often referred to as the "Westminster Abbey of the Pacific," is one of the oldest Christian places of worship in Hawaii. Constructed between 1836 and 1842, the church is built from coral blocks and served as the national church for the Hawaiian Kingdom and the site of many royal events.

Location: 957 Punchbowl Street, Honolulu, HI 96813

Getting There: Located in downtown Honolulu. Accessible by car, bus, or taxi/Uber.

Opening Time: Daily, 9:00 AM - 4:00 PM

Prices: Free to visit

Things to Do:
- Attend Sunday services
- Explore the historic cemetery
- Learn about the church's role in Hawaiian history

Contact/Booking Details:
- **Phone:** +1 808-522-1333
- **Website:** https://www.kawaiahao.org

Waikiki Beach: Surfing, Sunbathing, & Nightlife

Waikiki Beach may be one of the smallest strips of paradise on the island, but it delivers in the biggest of ways. Grace in the ocean means many things—for surfers, it's an opportunity for fun, and several breaks are spread out along this half-mile stretch at the base of Diamond Head and Fort DeRussy. For the first-time or beginner surfer, the gentle rollers are a hotspot for daredevils in the making. The wide, deep profiles and consistent breaks at Waikiki contribute to the large number of surfers in the water, so this beach is great for people-watching from the comfort of a comfortable lounger or beach towel in between paddleboarding lessons and a floating yoga class.

Interspersed with these rolling rides are the ancient traditions of our kūpuna, who navigated the Pacific by reading incoming swells as they were funneled into Waikiki. They called this "free energy," a renewable resource that glided all the way from Melanesia to shape Hawaiian history. What's more, Waikiki is home to some of the island's most luxurious hotels and vintage accommodations, and a slew of indoor and outdoor dining opportunities and essentially fabulous experiences to match. Whatever your reason for coming to Hawaii, Waikiki Beach quickly comes to mind. Expanding nearly two miles long from Kapahulu Pier to the cozy pockets of Condominium Row and beyond, this iconic coastline fronts some of the most cosmopolitan regulars and celebrities from around the world. And all its popularity is for good reason—it's simply fabulous! For starters, Waikiki isn't one beach—it's a lot of beaches rolled into one.

1 Waikiki Beach Walk

Description:
Waikiki Beach Walk is a vibrant, open-air promenade located in the heart of Waikiki, offering a mix of shops, restaurants, and entertainment venues. This area is perfect for strolling, shopping for local crafts, and dining with a view.

Location: 227 Lewers Street, Honolulu, HI 96815

Getting There: Easily accessible by foot if you're staying in Waikiki, or a short drive from other parts of Honolulu. Bus routes 8 and 20 serve the area.

Opening Time: Daily, 10:00 AM - 10:00 PM

Prices: Free entry; prices for dining and shopping vary.

Things to Do:
- Shop at local boutiques and global brands
- Dine at a variety of restaurants, from casual to upscale
- Enjoy live music and entertainment in the evenings

Contact/Booking Details:
🌐 **Website:** https://www.waikikibeachwalk.com

2 Duke Kahanamoku Statue

📄 Description:

The Duke Kahanamoku Statue honors the legendary Hawaiian surfer, Olympic swimmer, and the "Father of Modern Surfing." This statue is a must-visit landmark, celebrating Duke's contributions to popularizing surfing worldwide.

🗺 **Location:** Kalakaua Avenue, Honolulu, HI 96815

🚕 **Getting There:** Located on Waikiki Beach, easily accessible by foot or bus (Routes 8 and 20).

⏰ **Opening Time:** Always open

💳 **Prices:** Free to visit

Things to Do:
- Take photos with the iconic statue
- Learn about Duke Kahanamoku's life and achievements
- Enjoy the surrounding beach and ocean activities

Contact/Booking Details:
🌐 **Website:** https://www.honolulu.gov

3 Royal Hawaiian Hotel

📄 Description:

The Royal Hawaiian Hotel, also known as the "Pink Palace of the Pacific," is a historic luxury hotel that has been a Waikiki landmark since 1927. It offers luxurious accommodations and stunning beachfront views.

🗺 **Location:** 2259 Kalakaua Avenue, Honolulu, HI 96815

🚕 **Getting There:** Located in the heart of Waikiki, accessible by foot or a short drive.

🕑 **Opening Time:** Always open

💳 **Prices:** Room rates start at around $400 per night

Things to Do:
- Enjoy beachfront dining at the Mai Tai Bar
- Relax on the private beach
- Take part in traditional Hawaiian activities and lei-making classes

Contact/Booking Details:
☎ **Phone:** +1 808-923-7311
🌐 **Website:** https://www.royal-hawaiian.com

4 Moana Surfrider
📄 **Description:**
The Moana Surfrider, also known as the "First Lady of Waikiki," is the oldest hotel in Waikiki, established in 1901. It combines historic charm with modern luxury and offers a prime beachfront location.

📍 **Location:** 2365 Kalakaua Avenue, Honolulu, HI 96815

🚍 **Getting There:** Easily accessible by foot if you're staying in Waikiki, or by bus routes 8 and 20.

🕑 **Opening Time:** Always open

💳 **Prices:** Room rates start at around $350 per night

Things to Do:
- Enjoy afternoon tea on the veranda
- Relax in the Beach Bar under the iconic banyan tree
- Pamper yourself at the Moana Lani Spa

Contact/Booking Details:
☎ **Phone:** +1 808-922-3111

Website: https://www.moanasurfrider.com

5 Outrigger Waikiki Beach Resort

Description:
The Outrigger Waikiki Beach Resort offers modern amenities with traditional Hawaiian hospitality. It's known for its prime location and excellent dining options, including the famous Duke's Waikiki.

Location: 2335 Kalakaua Avenue, Honolulu, HI 96815

Getting There: Located directly on Waikiki Beach, accessible by foot or a short drive.

Opening Time: Always open

Prices: Room rates start at around $300 per night

Things to Do:
- Dine at Duke's Waikiki for beachfront dining
- Enjoy live Hawaiian music at the Hula Grill
- Relax by the beachfront pool

Contact/Booking Details:
Phone: +1 808-923-0711
Website: https://www.outrigger.com

Beach Scene and Water Sports
Waikiki Beach offers a vibrant beach scene with activities for everyone:

- Surfing: Waikiki is the birthplace of modern surfing. You can take surfing lessons or rent boards.
- Snorkeling: Explore underwater life at spots like Kuhio Beach and the Duke Kahanamoku Lagoon.
- Stand-Up Paddleboarding: Rent a paddleboard and explore the calm waters of Waikiki.

➡ Sunbathing: The stretch of sand along Waikiki Beach is perfect for sunbathing, especially near the Royal Hawaiian Hotel and Moana Surfrider.

Nightlife

Waikiki's nightlife is diverse, offering something for everyone:

➡ Bars and Clubs: Enjoy tropical cocktails and live music at venues like Mai Tai Bar and RumFire.
➡ Live Music and Shows: Experience Hawaiian music and hula performances at places like House Without a Key and Waikiki Beach Walk.

Chinatown & Culinary Scene: Food Tours & Local Eats

In Hawaii, one of the most densely populated blocks of the city is where all the magic happens. Four days a week, Market Day invites the public to sample different flavors, listen to live music, and engage all of their senses in the fun chaos that is downtown Honolulu. You can count on the latest installment of Chinatown pretty much anywhere, from green, market-only vendors to tucked-away alleys wedged in between bohemian local art and plenty of places to have a sit-down. If you've been to Asia and spotted an interesting street food trend, you'll likely find it in Chinatown. From Korean-stocked cans of Fritos to Thai food that you would have to fly 13 hours to have otherwise, and onto Chinese herbal vendors and Filipino dessert (with tons in between), you can indeed eat your way around the world here. And, since locals know what is good, enjoy these eats with a wide array of local craft beers offered at the Hops and Pops bar.

Chinatown is rife with fusion. In culturally rich Hawaii, we know that fusion is rarely without its merits. The Chinatown Cultural Plaza is an outdoor mall that has swallowed the corner of Maunakea and Hotel Streets. On Maunakea Street (at Marin), enjoy the Chinese New Year party (the date of which varies year to year). If you're crafty or just on the market for something unique, the Maunakea Marketplace is full to the brim with all the treasures of Chinatown. Open seven days a week, vendors change daily. Sip a bubble tea from numerous vendors, pick up a roast duck, or simply wander the maze of makeup, toys, and clothes which are sure to have you asking, "Who buys these things?" For a slice of a different culture void of what is often seen as the "obligatory geopolitical concoction," head on out to Honolulu's Historic Chinatown located in Honolulu, HI.

1 Chinatown Cultural Plaza
📑 Description:
Chinatown Cultural Plaza is a vibrant hub in Honolulu's Chinatown, offering a mix of retail shops, restaurants, and cultural activities. It's a great spot to experience the rich cultural diversity of Honolulu through its various shops and eateries.

📍 **Location:** 100 N Beretania Street, Honolulu, HI 96817

🚌 **Getting There:** Easily accessible by bus (Routes 1, 2, 3, and 13) or a short drive from Waikiki.

⏰ **Opening Time:** Daily, 9:00 AM - 10:00 PM

⊟ **Prices:** Free entry; prices for dining and shopping vary.

Things to Do:
- Shop for Asian goods and souvenirs
- Dine at local Chinese and Vietnamese restaurants
- Attend cultural performances and events

Contact/Booking Details:
⊕ **Website:** https://www.chinatownculturalplaza.com

2 Oahu Market
📑 **Description:**
Oahu Market is a bustling local market offering fresh produce, seafood, and traditional Asian groceries. It's an authentic place to experience local food culture and buy ingredients for homemade meals.

⚒ **Location:** 145 N King Street, Honolulu, HI 96817

🚌 **Getting There:** Accessible by bus (Routes 1, 2, 3, and 13) or a short drive from Waikiki.

⏰ **Opening Time:** Daily, 6:00 AM - 6:00 PM

⊟ **Prices:** Free entry; prices for goods vary.

Things to Do:
- Purchase fresh fruits, vegetables, and seafood
- Explore traditional Asian grocery items
- Enjoy local snacks and street food

Contact/Booking Details:
☎ **Phone:** +1 808-531-3007

3 Mei Sum Dim Sum
📄 **Description:**

Mei Sum Dim Sum is a popular restaurant in Chinatown known for its traditional Cantonese dim sum. It's a bustling spot with a casual atmosphere, perfect for enjoying a variety of small plates.

🏹 **Location:** 1170 Nuuanu Avenue #102, Honolulu, HI 96817

🚌 **Getting There:** Located in Chinatown, easily accessible by foot or bus (Routes 1, 2, 3, and 13).

⏰ **Opening Time:**
- Monday, Tuesday, Thursday, Friday: 9:00 AM - 8:00 PM
- Saturday, Sunday: 8:00 AM - 8:00 PM
- Closed on Wednesday
- 💳 **Prices:** Dishes typically range from $3 to $10

Things to Do:
- Enjoy a wide selection of dim sum
- Try specialties like shrimp dumplings and pork buns
- Experience traditional Cantonese dining

Contact/Booking Details:
- ☎ **Phone:** +1 808-531-3268
- 🌐 **Website:** https://www.meisumdimsum.com

4 The Pig and the Lady
📄 **Description:**

The Pig and the Lady is a renowned Vietnamese restaurant offering innovative dishes that blend traditional and modern flavors. It's known for its pho, creative cocktails, and vibrant atmosphere.

🏹 **Location:** 83 N King Street, Honolulu, HI 96817

🚌 **Getting There:** Located in Chinatown, accessible by foot or bus (Routes 1, 2, 3, and 13).

⏰ **Opening Time:**
- Tuesday - Saturday: 10:30 AM - 2:30 PM, 5:30 PM - 9:00 PM
- Sunday: 10:30 AM - 2:30 PM
- Closed on Monday

💳 **Prices:** Main dishes typically range from $12 to $25

Things to Do:
- Savor Vietnamese-inspired dishes like pho and banh mi
- Enjoy unique cocktails and desserts
- Experience a lively dining atmosphere

Contact/Booking Details:
☎ **Phone:** +1 808-585-8255
🌐 **Website:** https://www.thepigandthelady.com

5 Helena's Hawaiian Food
📄 **Description:**
Helena's Hawaiian Food is a beloved local restaurant serving traditional Hawaiian cuisine. It's an excellent place to experience authentic Hawaiian dishes like kalua pig, lomi salmon, and pipikaula short ribs.

📍 **Location:** 1240 N School Street, Honolulu, HI 96817

🚌 **Getting There:** Approximately a 10-minute drive from Waikiki; accessible by bus (Route 2).

⏰ **Opening Time:**
- Tuesday - Friday: 10:00 AM - 7:30 PM
- Closed on Saturday, Sunday, and Monday

💳 **Prices:** Main dishes typically range from $10 to $20

Things to Do:
- Enjoy traditional Hawaiian dishes
- Experience local hospitality
- Learn about Hawaiian culinary traditions

Contact/Booking Details:

☎ **Phone:** +1 808-845-8044

🌐 **Website:** https://www.helenashawaiianfood.com

Diamond Head: Iconic Hike & Panoramic Views

Often referred to as a dormant volcano, many people mistakenly believe that Diamond Head is a national park. The park takes up 475 coastal acres and is the site of a 300,000-year-old volcanic tuff cone, and is part of Diamond Head State Park. This geological wonder was formed after an underwater volcanic eruption and has been attracting curious visitors not only from Hawaii but from around the world. If your visit brings you to local beaches and/or to Waikiki, the odds are pretty good that you'll get a great view of Diamond Head.

Today, Diamond Head is a popular hiking destination for residents and visitors on Oahu. The crater spans the southeast coast of Oahu and is classified as a Military Reservation and National Natural Landmark. As a visitor to Oahu, you may begin to feel like you crave outdoor adventures. You crave the fresh air, you crave the stunning vistas, and you crave the satisfaction of the downhill cruise after a long hike. Sounds like you've caught the Diamond Head hiking bug. While it is not a national park, the crater does fall under the protection of the Hawaii State Parks system. History books show this natural history site was once called by an early explorer "tuff crater." With over 475 acres of total and 95 acres of developed lands, today you can experience a paved trail that takes you to this famous part of Diamond Head State Park. In fact, Diamond Head State Park was a vital part of an early comprehensive coastal defense system at the Diamond Head crater. Fun fact: a lighthouse stands atop Diamond Head today, above the crater interior.

1 Diamond Head State Monument
Description:
Diamond Head State Monument, known as "Leahi" in Hawaiian, is a volcanic tuff cone formed around 300,000 years ago. This iconic landmark is famous for its historic hiking trail, stunning coastal views, and significant military history. The name "Diamond Head" was given by British sailors in the 19th century who mistook the calcite crystals on the crater for diamonds.

Location: Diamond Head Road, Honolulu, HI 96815

Getting There:
➡ By Car: Approximately 10 minutes from Waikiki.
➡ By Bus: Routes 2 and 23.

⏰ **Opening Time:** Daily, 6:00 AM - 6:00 PM (last entry at 4:00 PM). Closed on Christmas and New Year's Day.

💳 **Prices:**
- ➡️ Entry Fee: $5 per pedestrian, $10 per vehicle.
- ➡️ Parking Fee: Included in the vehicle entry fee.
- ➡️ Hawaii Residents: Free with ID.

Tour Guide and Price:
- ➡️ Self-guided audio tour available for purchase online.
- ➡️ Guided tours provide historical and geological insights, priced around $25 to $50.

Things to Do:
- ➡️ Hike to the Summit: A 1.6-mile round trip with a moderately challenging trail featuring tunnels and bunkers. The summit offers panoramic views of Honolulu, Waikiki, and the Pacific Ocean.
- ➡️ Visitor Center: Learn about the crater's history, geology, and ecology.
- ➡️ Picnicking: Enjoy a picnic at the designated picnic pavilion after your hike.

Contact/Booking Details:
☎ **Phone:** +1 800-464-2924
🌐 **Website:** https://gostateparks.hawaii.gov/diamondhead/about

2 **Diamond Head Crater Hike**
📑 **Description:**
The Diamond Head Crater Hike is one of Oahu's most popular hiking trails. It offers a mix of geological and military history as you ascend to the summit. The trail was initially built in 1908 as part of Oahu's coastal defense system.

🔨 **Location:** Diamond Head Road, Honolulu, HI 96815

🚗 Getting There:
- ➡ By Car: Approximately 10 minutes from Waikiki.
- ➡ By Bus: Routes 2 and 23.

⏰ Opening Time: Daily, 6:00 AM - 6:00 PM (last entry at 4:00 PM). Closed on Christmas and New Year's Day.

💳 Prices:
- ➡ Entry Fee: $5 per pedestrian, $10 per vehicle.
- ➡ Parking Fee: Included in the vehicle entry fee.
- ➡ Hawaii Residents: Free with ID.

Tour Guide and Price:
- ➡ Self-guided audio tour available for purchase online.
- ➡ Guided tours offer detailed insights into the hike's historical significance, priced around $25 to $50.

Things to Do:
- ➡ Hiking: The 1.6-mile round trip hike to the summit provides breathtaking views of the island. The hike includes a steep ascent, tunnels, and a final climb up a spiral staircase.
- ➡ Photography: Capture panoramic views from the summit, including the coastline and the cityscape of Honolulu.
- ➡ Learn History: Explore the military bunkers and Fire Control Station at the summit, which directed artillery fire during the early 1900s.

Contact/Booking Details:
- ☎ Phone: +1 800-464-2924
- 🌐 Website: https://gostateparks.hawaii.gov/diamondhead/about

Arts & Culture: Bishop Museum, Art Galleries, & Live Music

As the largest city in the state, Honolulu is the main hub for some of the best creative and cultural endeavors in the Pacific. In fact, with mere moments of exploration, you will understand Honolulu to be uniquely Honolulu: a bolstering force that drives Hawaii's arts scene. Architectural oddities like Fern Grotto symbolize the late 1930s embrace of technology and tourism, while John Melville's bronze work "Aloha Hawaii" suggests post-WWII longing for a simpler and more tropical time. As former PRIDE programs coordinator Emily Hope Smith puts it: "Residents and visitors alike will surely gain insights into the mindset of past generations of those who have inherited Honolulu and feel the aloha that is Hawaii."

Honolulu inspires not only gallant windows into the past but also harbors premier accounts of multiculturalism that tourists and residents visit local and national institutions alike to experience the complexity of Hawaiian history and contemporary life. From the crown jewels of the Bishop Museum, including monumental Ni'ihau necklaces made from whale ivory, to a 7,000-square-foot grove of po, or sacred ladders used to access the temples at the Pu'uhonua o

Hōnaunau National Historical Park, visitors can gain insights into the aesthetics, spiritual practices, and values of Hawaii. While the Ho'oulu Mele Writing, Performing, and Recording Project at the park examines contemporary Hawaiian poetic expression and builds a bridge between ancient and modern musical traditions, fine arts like music, painting, and quilting feature vessels of ancient to present-day Hawaiian artisanship.

1 Bishop Museum

Description:

The Bernice Pauahi Bishop Museum, founded in 1889, is the largest museum in Hawaii and holds a vast collection of Hawaiian artifacts and royal family heirlooms. It serves as a cultural and natural history museum, showcasing the history and culture of Hawaii and other Pacific islands.

Location: 1525 Bernice Street, Honolulu, HI 96817

Getting There: Approximately 10 minutes by car from downtown Honolulu; accessible by bus (Route 2).

Opening Time: Daily, 9:00 AM - 5:00 PM

Prices:
- Adults: $24.95
- Seniors (65+): $21.95
- Children (4-17): $16.95
- Hawaii residents and military discounts available

Things to Do:
- Explore Hawaiian Hall, showcasing ancient Hawaiian artifacts
- Visit the Science Adventure Center for interactive exhibits
- Attend planetarium shows

Contact/Booking Details:
- **Phone:** +1 808-847-3511

🌐 **Website:** https://www.bishopmuseum.org

---

2 Honolulu Museum of Art
📑 **Description:**
The Honolulu Museum of Art is home to an impressive collection of Asian, Western, and Pacific art. It was founded in 1927 and offers a diverse range of exhibits, including contemporary art and traditional Hawaiian pieces.

🪧 **Location:** 900 S Beretania Street, Honolulu, HI 96814

🚌 **Getting There:** Located in downtown Honolulu, accessible by car or bus (Routes 1, 2, 4, and 6).

⏰ **Opening Time:**
- Tuesday - Saturday: 10:00 AM - 6:00 PM
- Sunday: 10:00 AM - 6:00 PM
- Closed on Mondays

💳 **Prices:**
- Adults: $20
- Seniors (62+): $10
- Children (18 and under): Free
- Hawaii residents: $10

Things to Do:
- Tour various art collections and exhibitions
- Attend art classes and workshops
- Enjoy the Doris Duke Theatre for films and lectures

Contact/Booking Details:
☎ **Phone:** +1 808-532-8700
🌐 **Website:** https://www.honolulumuseum.org

3 Hawaii Theatre Center
Description:
The Hawaii Theatre, known as the "Pride of the Pacific," has been a cultural cornerstone since 1922. This beautifully restored venue hosts a variety of performances, including concerts, plays, and dance shows, and is recognized for its architectural elegance.

Location: 1130 Bethel Street, Honolulu, HI 96813

Getting There: Located in downtown Honolulu, accessible by car or bus.

Opening Time: Box Office: Monday - Friday, 10:00 AM - 4:00 PM

Prices: Ticket prices vary by event.

Things to Do:
- Attend live performances ranging from music to theater
- Participate in docent-led tours to learn about the theater's history and architecture
- Enjoy special events and educational programs

Contact/Booking Details:
Phone: Box Office: +1 808-528-0506, Admin Office: +1 808-791-1397
Website: https://www.hawaiitheatre.com

4 Blue Note Hawaii
Description:
Blue Note Hawaii is a premier jazz club located in the Outrigger Waikiki Beach Resort. It features live performances from top local and international artists in an intimate setting, perfect for music lovers.

Location: 2335 Kalakaua Avenue, Honolulu, HI 96815

🚌 **Getting There:** Located in Waikiki, easily accessible by foot or bus (Routes 2 and 13).

⏰ **Opening Time:** Showtimes vary; typically, performances are scheduled for evenings.

💳 **Prices:** Ticket prices vary by event, typically ranging from $25 to $45.

Things to Do:
➡ Enjoy live jazz, blues, and Hawaiian music performances
➡ Dine and drink during shows with a full menu available
➡ Experience special events and artist meet-and-greets

Contact/Booking Details:
☎ **Phone:** +1 808-777-4890
🌐 **Website:** https://www.bluenotehawaii.com

---

5 **Shangri La Museum of Islamic Art, Culture & Design**
📑 **Description:**
Shangri La, the former estate of heiress Doris Duke, is a museum dedicated to Islamic art, culture, and design. The museum houses an extensive collection of artifacts from countries such as Iran, India, and Morocco, and is renowned for its beautiful architecture and gardens.

🔨 **Location:** 4055 Papu Circle, Honolulu, HI 96816

🚌 **Getting There:** Approximately 20 minutes by car from downtown Honolulu; visitors must take a shuttle from the Honolulu Museum of Art.

⏰ **Opening Time:**
Thursday - Saturday: Tour times at 9:00 AM, 10:00 AM, and 1:30 PM
Closed Sunday - Wednesday

Prices:
- Adults: $25 (includes admission to Honolulu Museum of Art)
- Seniors (65+): $20
- Children (under 12): Not permitted

Things to Do:
- Guided tours of the estate and art collection
- Explore the beautiful gardens and architectural details
- Learn about Doris Duke's life and her passion for Islamic art

Contact/Booking Details:
- **Phone:** +1 808-532-3853
- **Website:** https://www.shangrilahawaii.org

Beyond Honolulu

In truth, Oahu is not Honolulu. Land mass doesn't really favor one region or another, but culturally and experientially, it's not an even split. Honolulu is a hub of activity, teeming with people who travel from around the world to enjoy the thrill of 5-star dining, beautiful shopping, and a colossal collection of attractions that represent the entire sweep of Hawaii luxury. There is no catch to the concept of visiting Waikiki, but just like in Rome and Paris, to only step out of one's hotel in Honolulu is to leave the rest of the island an unknown and mostly unexplored dream. With the day-by-day guide to Oahu that begins on page 26, this guide recommits you to the idea of not just living it up in luxury at its most luxurious, but of working your way week-to-week across the island to track down new adventures, new locals, new wilderness, and the surprisingly large number of places where side street culinary treasures still marinate in forbidden and genuine flavors. And, of course, because this is Hawaii, they await at every turn.

Waianae still bears up the west coast of the island and the Leeward side runs past a few regions that are as easy to find as they are breathtaking to consider. Kapolei is the west coast's home for the largest and most decadent resorts, from the Marriott to the Ko Olina Beach Villas and, somewhat further down the beach, Ocean Tower. There isn't much diversity between the three, though Ocean Tower holds our esteem (and more to the point, has our esteem holding upper floor units, which, dammit people, give you such a view) as a stopover or even just a destination all of its own. Your dollar is golden at Marriott's timeshare island, but Ko Olina is generally expensive enough to prove Preferred. Ko Olina's attractions are so pronounced and inviting that they could practically suffice as a stand-in for the island tour themes this supplement explores in depth. For those with the right amount of time or island to go around, Olelo suggests both the Paradise Cove Luau and the Ko Olina Golf Club, one of the best on the way out to the sandy west coast.

North Shore: Surfing Meccas (Pipeline, Sunset Beach) & Laid-Back Towns

The North Shore of Oahu is where you will find world-class surfing during the winter months. Everyone knows about places like Pipeline and Sunset Beach and how scary and amazing this stretch of coastline can be. Driving along this part of Kamehameha Highway leaves no doubt as to why it's taken on a larger-than-life reputation. There are oversized waves kicking up multiple stories of sea spray, and flocks of surf photographers jockeying for the perfect vantage point.

The same goes for the surfers, desperate to catch one (or a few) to end all waves. This is one of the main hubs of surfing in the world, after all. Most of the time, all that surf-induced intensity just results in people watching. Scattered along the coastline of Haleiwa, Waimea Bay, Sunset Beach, and Velzyland, and stretched down to Waialua, you'll find a series of laid-back towns that are the exact opposite of all that adrenaline-pumping action. Life on the North Shore is anything but fast-paced, especially once summer rolls around. Driving the 28 scenic miles, aka highways 930 and 83, that make up the North Shore portion of Kamehameha Highway takes about an hour, give or take. But honestly, who's in a hurry? Longing for a little action? If you simply must get your fix of hunter-gatherer action, definitely consider a spearfishing tour. Just imagine: you, a spear, an emerald sea, and a haul of fresh fish at the end of the day.

1 Banzai Pipeline
Description:
The Banzai Pipeline, located at Ehukai Beach, is one of the most famous surf spots in the world, known for its massive, barreling waves that attract top surfers globally. It's a legendary location for professional surfing competitions, particularly during the winter months.

Location: Ehukai Beach, 9-337 Ke Nui Road, Haleiwa, HI 96712

Getting There:
- By Car: Approximately a 1-hour drive from Honolulu via H-1 and Kamehameha Highway.
- By Bus: Routes 60 and 88A from Waikiki to Haleiwa.

Opening Time: Always open

📇 **Prices:** Free to visit

Things to Do:

➡ Surf Watching: Observe professional surfers tackle the powerful waves, especially during competitions like the Triple Crown of Surfing.

➡ Beach Activities: Enjoy sunbathing, beachcombing, and picnicking.

➡ Photography: Capture stunning action shots of surfers and scenic beach views.

Contact/Booking Details:

🌐 **Website:** https://gohawaii.com

2 Sunset Beach

📑 **Description:**

Sunset Beach is renowned for its breathtaking sunsets and excellent surfing conditions. It is part of the North Shore's "Seven-Mile Miracle," a stretch of coastline known for its surf breaks.

🪓 **Location:** 59-104 Kamehameha Highway, Haleiwa, HI 96712

🚙 **Getting There:**

➡ By Car: About 1-hour drive from Honolulu.

➡ By Bus: Routes 60 and 88A.

⏰ **Opening Time:** Always open

📇 **Prices:** Free to visit

Things to Do:

➡ Surfing: Best for experienced surfers, especially during winter.

➡ Sunbathing: Relax on the expansive sandy beach.

➡ Sunset Viewing: Enjoy stunning sunsets over the Pacific Ocean.

Contact/Booking Details:

🌐 **Website:** https://gohawaii.com

---

3 **Waimea Bay Beach Park**

📑 **Description:**

Waimea Bay is famous for its big wave surfing in the winter and calm waters in the summer. It's a popular spot for cliff diving, snorkeling, and swimming.

📍 **Location:** 61-031 Kamehameha Highway, Haleiwa, HI 96712

🚌 **Getting There:**

➡ By Car: About 1-hour drive from Honolulu.
➡ By Bus: Routes 60 and 88A.

⏰ **Opening Time:** Always open

🎟 **Prices:** Free to visit

Things to Do:

➡ Big Wave Surfing: Watch surfers tackle some of the largest waves in the world during winter.
➡ Swimming and Snorkeling: Enjoy the calm waters in the summer.
➡ Cliff Diving: For the adventurous, Waimea Bay is known for its jumping rock.

Contact/Booking Details:

🌐 **Website:** https://gohawaii.com

---

4 Haleiwa Town

📑 **Description:**

Haleiwa is a charming town known for its surf culture, boutique shops, art galleries, and diverse dining options. It's the gateway to the North Shore.

📍 **Location:** Haleiwa, HI 96712

🚕 **Getting There:**
➡ By Car: About 45 minutes from Honolulu.
➡ By Bus: Routes 52, 55, and 88A.

⏰ **Opening Time:** Shops and restaurants typically open from 10:00 AM to 6:00 PM.

💳 **Prices:** Varies by activity and establishment.

Things to Do:
➡ Shopping: Browse local boutiques and surf shops.
➡ Dining: Enjoy local food at eateries like Matsumoto Shave Ice and Haleiwa Joe's.
➡ Art Galleries: Visit galleries showcasing local art and crafts.

Contact/Booking Details:
🌐 **Website:** https://haleiwatown.com

5 **Polynesian Cultural Center**
📑 **Description:**
The Polynesian Cultural Center offers an immersive experience into the cultures of Polynesia, with villages representing Samoa, Tahiti, Fiji, Tonga, Hawaii, and Aotearoa (New Zealand).

📍 **Location:** 55-370 Kamehameha Highway, Laie, HI 96762

🚕 **Getting There:**
➡ By Car: About 1-hour drive from Honolulu.
➡ By Bus: Routes 55 and 60.

⏰ **Opening Time:**
Monday - Saturday, 12:45 PM - 9:00 PM.
Closed on Sundays.

Prices:
- General Admission: Starting at $64.95
- Packages: Various options with activities and dining included.

Things to Do:
- Cultural Exhibits: Explore the villages and learn about different Polynesian cultures.
- Luau: Enjoy a traditional Hawaiian feast and entertainment.
- Evening Show: Watch "Ha: Breath of Life," a Polynesian revue.

Contact/Booking Details:
- ☎ **Phone:** +1 800-367-7060
- ⊕ **Website:** https://www.polynesia.com

6 Turtle Bay Resort
📑 Description:
Turtle Bay Resort is a premier destination offering luxury accommodations, golf courses, and numerous activities on Oahu's North Shore. It's a perfect spot for relaxation and adventure.

Location: 57-091 Kamehameha Highway, Kahuku, HI 96731

🚌 Getting There:
- By Car: About 1-hour drive from Honolulu.
- By Bus: Routes 60 and 88A.

⏰ Opening Time: Always open

Prices: Room rates start at $350 per night

Things to Do:
- Golfing: Play on two championship golf courses.
- Horseback Riding: Explore trails with ocean views.
- Water Sports: Surfing, stand-up paddleboarding, and kayaking.

Contact/Booking Details:

☎ **Phone:** +1 808-293-6000

🌐 **Website:** https://www.turtlebayresort.com

Windward Coast: Lush Valleys (Kualoa Ranch), Scenic Drives, & Hikes

The Windward Coast of Oʻahu - a series of lush, green valleys that punctuate the sheer Koʻolau, framed by arcs of sandy coastline - is a wondrous place. There are a host of picturesque, must-see activities: a stunning scenic drive; a chance for non-hikers to experience one of my favorite vistas on the island (Kualoa Regional Park); and a short, easy hike to one waterfall and a more strenuous hike to a second soaring waterfall up a stunning, deep, lush valley.

Oahu's Windward Coast is special. Many people come to Oahu without venturing onto the Windward (east) side of the island, yet it is the heart of Oahu for many locals. The shoreline is long and the background of this coastline is nothing short of picturesque, especially here in the northern reaches. You can drive straight through the Windward side in a racing-blink-of-the-eye fashion on KH1, an expressway that runs straight through the valley formed by the Ko'olau Mountain Range and the Koolau Gap. You'll cruise past military bases, small towns, and the Koolau mountains on your right and the sheer, verdant drop-off mountains on your left. This area has been featured in many movies, including "50 First Dates" with Adam Sandler; "Blue Crush"; "George of the Jungle"; "Pearl Harbor"; "Godzilla"; and "Jurassic Park." In fact, the towering, green Koolau Mountain Range plays the part of the rest of "the Land That Time Forgot" in the television show "LOST," symbolizing its wilderness and power. The lush valley specked with green, irresistible allure is no trick photography. It's the Kualoa Ranch on Oahu's Windward side. It's a huge slice of paradise - just ask Tinseltown.

1 Kualoa Ranch
Description:
Kualoa Ranch is a 4,000-acre private nature reserve and working cattle ranch, famous for its stunning landscapes and numerous movie filming locations, including "Jurassic Park" and "Lost". It offers a variety of tours and activities, from horseback riding to UTV adventures.

Location: 49-560 Kamehameha Highway, Kaneohe, HI 96744

Getting There:
- By Car: Approximately a 45-minute drive from Honolulu.
- By Shuttle: Available from Waikiki hotels for an additional fee.

Opening Time: Daily, 7:30 AM - 6:00 PM

Prices:
- Hollywood Movie Sites Tour: $58 per adult
- Jurassic Adventure Tour: $176 per adult
- UTV Raptor Tour: $179 per adult

Things to Do:
- Hollywood Movie Sites Tour: Visit iconic filming locations.
- Jurassic Adventure Tour: Explore the ranch's valleys on a 4WD tour.
- UTV Raptor Tour: Drive through the ranch's scenic landscapes.
- Farm & Cultural Tours: Learn about the ranch's agricultural practices and Hawaiian culture.

Contact/Booking Details:
☎ **Phone:** +1 808-237-7321
🌐 **Website:** https://www.kualoa.com

---

2 Nuuanu Pali Lookout
📝 **Description:**
Nuuanu Pali Lookout offers breathtaking views of the Windward Coast and is historically significant as the site of the Battle of Nuuanu, where King Kamehameha I won a decisive victory to unite the Hawaiian Islands.

📍 **Location:** Nuuanu Pali Drive, Honolulu, HI 96817

🚕 **Getting There:**
By Car: Approximately a 30-minute drive from Honolulu.

⏰ **Opening Time:** Daily, 6:00 AM - 6:00 PM

💳 **Prices:** Free to visit

Things to Do:
- Sightseeing: Enjoy panoramic views of the Windward Coast.
- Photography: Capture stunning landscapes and historical markers.

Contact/Booking Details:
🌐 **Website:** https://gohawaii.com

3 Byodo-In Temple
📑 **Description:**
The Byodo-In Temple is a replica of a 900-year-old Buddhist temple in Uji, Japan. It was established in 1968 to commemorate the 100th anniversary of Japanese immigrants arriving in Hawaii. The temple is set against a lush, green backdrop and offers a peaceful retreat.

📍 **Location:** 47-200 Kahekili Highway, Kaneohe, HI 96744

🚗 **Getting There:**
By Car: Approximately a 35-minute drive from Honolulu.

⏰ **Opening Time:** Daily, 8:30 AM - 4:30 PM

💳 **Prices:**
- General Admission: $5
- Seniors: $4
- Children: $2

Things to Do:
- Temple Visit: Explore the serene grounds and ring the Peace Bell.
- Pond: Feed the koi fish and see black swans.
- Meditation: Enjoy the tranquil surroundings for meditation and reflection.

Contact/Booking Details:
☎ **Phone:** +1 808-239-8811
🌐 **Website:** https://byodo-in.com

4 Ho'omaluhia Botanical Garden
📑 **Description:**
Ho'omaluhia Botanical Garden spans 400 acres and features plants from tropical regions around the world. The garden's name means "to make a place of peace and tranquility," reflecting its serene atmosphere.

Location: 45-680 Luluku Road, Kaneohe, HI 96744

Getting There:
By Car: Approximately a 30-minute drive from Honolulu.

Opening Time: Daily, 9:00 AM - 4:00 PM

Prices: Free to visit

Things to Do:
- Walking Trails: Explore the diverse plant collections.
- Picnicking: Enjoy a picnic with scenic views.
- Fishing: Catch and release fishing in the garden's lake (weekends only).

Contact/Booking Details:
Phone: +1 808-233-7323
Website: https://www.honolulu.gov

5 Lanikai Pillbox Hike
Description:
The Lanikai Pillbox Hike, also known as the Kaiwa Ridge Trail, offers stunning views of the Mokulua Islands, Lanikai Beach, and Kailua. It's a popular trail for both locals and tourists, providing a moderately challenging hike with rewarding vistas.

Location: Lanikai, Kailua, HI 96734

Getting There:
By Car: Approximately a 40-minute drive from Honolulu.

Opening Time: Always open

Prices: Free to visit

Things to Do:
- Hiking: Enjoy a 1.8-mile round-trip hike with panoramic views.
- Photography: Capture breathtaking landscapes and sunrise views.
- Historical Exploration: Visit the WWII-era pillbox bunkers along the trail.

Contact/Booking Details:
- Website: https://gohawaii.com

Leeward Coast: Ko Olina Resort, Water Sports, & Polynesian Cultural Center

After enjoying the North Shore, we now head to the Leeward Coast, joining Farrington Highway to continue circling the island. This is a smaller, quicker section and includes passing through the town of Waianae. Although Waianae, unfortunately, does have a relatively high crime rate, the residents have done a good job of building a beautiful park at Kahe Point, which includes a monument and a small museum. Further down the road, you will find the four "resort" lagoons of the Ko Olina Resort (Ager, Green, White, and Black Lagoons). They're separated by long, treeless mountains, with little man-made beaches and lounging areas on the sand. The tiny beaches make the water close by, clean and clear. The lagoons were made even more stunning after a 2017 renovation in which the brackish estuary - martian - was restored. Tourists drink at the bar and sleep, float, or snorkel, while peacocks and their peahen flock roam. The Marriott hotel joined the newly refurbished Four Seasons resort in 2016 to be the second luxury asset here and first.

Water Sports and Polynesian Cultural Center
There are also a ton of family-friendly water sports. Visitors have the chance to participate and to ride behind any of these water sports boat rentals for a fee. Most renters give a ticket with all the amenities. The star boats are equipped with slides for a fun time in the water. As you make your way around the island, don't miss a chance to see the Polynesian Cultural Center. It's at the end of the main highway! Even though there are many activities you may partake in, including wilderness tours and nighttime shows, many people only go there for the food and to purchase some inexpensive Pasifika souvenirs, jams, and gandules. The spa has also collaborated with a candle company, a soap company that uses veggie blends, and herbal supplements.

1 **Ko Olina Resort**
Description:
Ko Olina Resort is a luxurious beachfront community featuring world-class accommodations, dining, and recreational activities. It includes four pristine lagoons, the Aulani Disney Resort, and the Four Seasons Resort.

Location: 92-1480 Aliinui Drive, Kapolei, HI 96707

Getting There:
By Car: Approximately 30 minutes from Honolulu via H-1 West.

⏰ **Opening Time:** Always open

💳 **Prices:** Varies by activity and establishment

Things to Do:
- Beach Activities: Enjoy the tranquil lagoons for swimming, snorkeling, and paddleboarding.
- Golfing: Play at the Ko Olina Golf Club.
- Dining: Explore numerous restaurants and bars within the resort.

Contact/Booking Details:
- ☎ **Phone:** +1 808-676-7695
- 🌐 **Website:** https://www.koolina.com

2 Paradise Cove Luau

📝 **Description:**

Paradise Cove Luau offers a traditional Hawaiian luau experience with a beachfront setting, featuring cultural demonstrations, a buffet dinner, and Polynesian performances.

🔨 **Location:** 92-1089 Aliinui Drive, Kapolei, HI 96707

🚗 **Getting There:**
- By Car: About 30 minutes from Honolulu via H-1 West.
- By Shuttle: Transportation from Waikiki available with certain packages.

⏰ **Opening Time:** Daily, 5:00 PM - 9:00 PM

💳 **Prices:**
- Standard Luau Package: $125 per adult
- Deluxe Luau Package: $175 per adult

Things to Do:
- Cultural Activities: Participate in traditional Hawaiian games and crafts.
- Buffet Dinner: Enjoy a Hawaiian feast featuring local dishes.
- Polynesian Show: Watch hula and fire-knife performances.

Contact/Booking Details:
- ☎ **Phone:** +1 808-842-5911
- ⊕ **Website:** https://www.paradisecove.com

3 Wet'n'Wild Hawaii

📑 **Description:**

Wet'n'Wild Hawaii is a water park offering a variety of attractions for all ages, including water slides, wave pools, and lazy rivers. It's a great destination for family fun and adventure.

📍 **Location:** 400 Farrington Highway, Kapolei, HI 96707

🚕 **Getting There:**
- By Car: Approximately 30 minutes from Honolulu via H-1 West.
- By Bus: Route 40.

⏰ **Opening Time:** Daily, 10:30 AM - 4:00 PM (hours may vary seasonally)

🖼 **Prices:**
- General Admission: $49.99 per person
- Discounted Rates: Available for children, seniors, and military

Things to Do:
- Water Slides: Enjoy rides like the Tornado, Shaka, and Waianae Coaster.
- Wave Pool: Relax in the Hawaiian Waters Wave Pool.
- Lazy River: Float along the Kapolei Kooler.

Contact/Booking Details:
☎ **Phone:** +1 808-674-9283
🌐 **Website:** https://www.wetnwildhawaii.com

---

4 Kapolei
📑 **Description:**
Kapolei, known as Oahu's "Second City," offers shopping, dining, and entertainment options. It's a growing urban center with a blend of modern amenities and natural beauty.

📍 **Location:** Kapolei, HI 96707

🚗 **Getting There:**
➡ By Car: About 30 minutes from Honolulu via H-1 West.
➡ By Bus: Routes 40, 40A, and 93.

Things to Do:
➡ Shopping: Visit Ka Makana Ali'i for a variety of retail stores and restaurants.
➡ Dining: Enjoy diverse dining options from local Hawaiian cuisine to international fare.
➡ Recreation: Explore local parks and recreational facilities.

Contact/Booking Details:
🌐 **Website:** https://gokapolei.com

---

5 Coral Crater Adventure Park
📑 **Description:**
Coral Crater Adventure Park is an outdoor adventure center offering thrilling activities such as ziplining, ATV rides, and a challenging aerial obstacle course. It's a perfect destination for adrenaline seekers.

📍 **Location:** 91-1780 Midway Street, Kapolei, HI 96707

🚗 **Getting There:**
➡ By Car: Approximately 30 minutes from Honolulu via H-1 West.

➡ By Shuttle: Transportation from Waikiki available with certain packages.

🕐 **Opening Time:** Daily, 8:00 AM - 6:00 PM

💳 **Prices:**
➡ Zipline Tour: Starting at $99.99 per person
➡ ATV Adventure: Starting at $149.99 per person
➡ Ultimate Adventure Package: $399.99 per person

Things to Do:
➡ Ziplining: Experience the thrill of multiple zip lines through the park.
➡ ATV Rides: Navigate off-road trails on a guided ATV tour.
➡ Adventure Tower: Conquer climbing walls and take a 50-foot free fall.

Contact/Booking Details:
☎ **Phone:** +1 808-626-5773
🌐 **Website:** https://coralcrater.com

CHAPTER 3: BIG ISLAND: ISLAND OF FIRE AND ICE

This easternmost island is a distinct geological character. On the air, its lava airfields are broken only by Mauna Loa and Mauna Kea, the islands' two highest mountains. From the land, its southeastern coastline slopes west, interrupted by five massive shield magma domes. The inexorable eastern progress of the Pacific Ridge and the western retreat of the Hawaiian "hot spot" created the island of Hawaii.

The tallest mountains on Earth penetrate the resilient island crust by as much as 19,700 meters (6.4 km on land and 13,100 km below adjacent seafloor); the weight of these massive volcanoes push the lithosphere downward and causes their mass to slowly sink into the mantle. The shield of lava accumulations is dotted with more than fifty cinder cones from smaller, more incremental eruptions. Not surprisingly, this remarkable convergence of volcanic activity and forces led to six periods of eruption in the past 200 years: two in the mid-1800s, three in the early 1900s, and one, ongoing, from 1983 to the present.

The history of island building leaves additional traces. Where a new island of Hawaii rose from the sea floor to its greatest height, succeeding aerial lava flows and ocean wave remaking the land have carved steep cliffs on the southeastern, southwestern, and northern-facing slopes. Finally, Kahoolawe, devoid of high peaks because of the smaller lava pile accumulated here, was too small to carry the great weight of mass into which much of its subsurface had been converted; having little resistance to the downwelling of the Pacific plate beneath us.

The Big Island of Hawaii is one of a kind in the world of travel due to its unbelievable geology. This single island is made up of five volcanoes, still actively shaping and reforming the island, and even its name "the Big Island" is an attempt to encompass its not easily manageable size.

Volcanoes National Park: Witnessing Creation

Visiting Hawai'i Island - also known as the Big Island - is like stepping back in time and forwards into the raw existence of Earth. Never has this been more literal than in the depth of Hawaii Volcanoes National Park (HVNP) and the Kilauea Caldera, the central point of activity for the national park. This park is unique in many ways and worth days of exploration not only for its beauty but also its historical significance and its geology.

Though visitable 287 days a year (or 79% of the calendar year), the Kilauea Volcano itself serves as a beacon to the island from the south side. Vents as recent as 2018 have pitted farmland and eaten away at landmarks as cliffs have been created or pushed back inland. In the evening, plumes of vapors and fumes may be all you see. As the evening grows, a red or pink glow will become increasingly easier to see, until you can't help but linger at the edge of the caldera. Watching the slow but intense rivers of lava will lull you into contemplation of how small and inconsequential our works and worries truly are. The lava shifts back and forth; forever changing the shape of the island in a matter of years at a rate we are not used to contemplating. Only the relieved hiss of steam marks the flows' passing. In the center of it all, the Halema'uma'u Crater's walls glow brighter as night darkens. In its center, spatter and lava pool in an arcane and fitting measurement of time's passage in the brittle islands.

1 Kīlauea Caldera

Description:

Kīlauea Caldera is a massive crater formed by the collapse of the summit of Kīlauea Volcano, one of the most active volcanoes in the world. It has a long history of eruptions, with the most recent major eruption occurring in 2018, which dramatically altered the landscape and doubled the size of Halemaʻumaʻu Crater.

Location: Hawaiʻi Volcanoes National Park, HI 96718

Getting There:

By Car: Approximately 45 minutes from Hilo via Highway 11.

Opening Time: Always open

Prices:
- Private vehicle: $30 (valid for seven days)
- Motorcycle: $25 (valid for seven days)
- Individual pedestrian/bicycle: $15 (valid for seven days)

Things to Do:
- Hiking: Explore trails around the caldera.
- Viewpoints: Visit Kīlauea Overlook for panoramic views.
- Photography: Capture the dramatic landscapes.

Contact/Booking Details:
☎ **Phone:** +1 808-985-6011
🌐 **Website:** https://www.nps.gov/havo/index.htm

② Thurston Lava Tube (Nahuku)
📑 **Description:**
The Thurston Lava Tube is a large, walkable lava tube formed by flowing lava that cooled and left a hollow tunnel. It is approximately 600 feet long and provides a fascinating glimpse into volcanic processes.

📍 **Location:** Hawai'i Volcanoes National Park, HI 96718

🚗 **Getting There:**
By Car: Park at the Kīlauea Iki Trailhead or Devastation Trail parking lot.

⏰ **Opening Time:** Always open

💳 **Prices:** Included in park entrance fee

Things to Do:
➡ Walking: Walk through the illuminated lava tube.
➡ Nature Viewing: Enjoy the surrounding rainforest.

Contact/Booking Details:
☎ **Phone:** +1 808-985-6011
🌐 **Website:** https://www.nps.gov/havo/index.htm

③ Chain of Craters Road
📑 **Description:**
Chain of Craters Road is an 18.8-mile scenic drive that descends from the summit of Kīlauea to the coast, passing through varied landscapes including volcanic craters and lava flows.

📍 **Location:** Hawai'i Volcanoes National Park, HI 96718

🚗 **Getting There:**
By Car: Enter the park via Highway 11 and follow the signs.

⏰ **Opening Time:** Always open

💳 **Prices:** Included in park entrance fee

Things to Do:
➡ Scenic Drive: Enjoy the changing landscapes and stop at viewpoints.
➡ Hiking: Explore trails along the route.
➡ Photography: Capture the dramatic volcanic features.

Contact/Booking Details:
☎ **Phone:** +1 808-985-6011
🌐 **Website:** https://www.nps.gov/havo/index.htm

4 **Jaggar Museum**
📝 **Description:**
Jaggar Museum, located near the Kīlauea Caldera, offers exhibits on volcanology, Hawaiian culture, and the park's unique geology. Note: As of recent updates, the museum is temporarily closed due to damage from volcanic activity.

📍 **Location:** Hawai'i Volcanoes National Park, HI 96718

🚗 **Getting There:**
By Car: Near the Kīlauea Overlook on Crater Rim Drive.
⏰ **Opening Time:** Currently closed for repairs

💳 **Prices:** Included in park entrance fee

Things to Do:
➡ Educational Exhibits: Learn about volcanic activity.
➡ Viewpoints: Enjoy views from the nearby overlook.

Contact/Booking Details:
☎ **Phone:** +1 808-985-6011
🌐 **Website:** https://www.nps.gov/havo/index.htm

5 Steam Vents
📑 **Description:**
The Steam Vents, also known as Haʻakulamanu, are areas where volcanic gases escape through cracks in the ground, creating a unique and otherworldly landscape.

📍 **Location:** Hawaiʻi Volcanoes National Park, HI 96718

🚗 **Getting There:**
By Car: Near the Kīlauea Visitor Center.
⏰ **Opening Time:** Always open

💳 **Prices:** Included in park entrance fee

Things to Do:
➡ Walking: Short trails lead to steam vents.
➡ Photography: Capture the steamy, surreal scenery.

Contact/Booking Details:
☎ **Phone:** +1 808-985-6011
🌐 **Website:** https://www.nps.gov/havo/index.htm

6 Devastation Trail
📑 **Description:**
Devastation Trail is a paved, easy trail that traverses a stark landscape created by the 1959 eruption of Kīlauea Iki. The area was buried in cinders, creating an almost lunar environment.

📍 **Location:** Hawai'i Volcanoes National Park, HI 96718

🚗 **Getting There:**
By Car: Near the Kīlauea Iki Crater.
⏰ **Opening Time:** Always open

💳 **Prices:** Included in park entrance fee

Things to Do:
➡ Hiking: A 1-mile round-trip walk.
➡ Nature Viewing: See how life is gradually returning to the area.

Contact/Booking Details:
☎ **Phone:** +1 808-985-6011
🌐 **Website:** https://www.nps.gov/havo/index.htm

7️⃣ **Kīlauea Iki Crater**
📄 **Description:**
Kīlauea Iki Crater was the site of a dramatic eruption in 1959 that sent fountains of lava 1,900 feet into the air. Today, you can hike across the crater floor and see the remnants of this powerful volcanic event.

📍 **Location:** Hawai'i Volcanoes National Park, HI 96718

🚗 **Getting There:**

By Car: Park at the Kīlauea Iki Trailhead.
⏰ **Opening Time:** Always open

💳 **Prices:** Included in park entrance fee

Things to Do:
➡ Hiking: The 4-mile Kīlauea Iki Trail takes you across the crater floor.

➡ Viewpoints: Overlook the crater from the rim trail.

Contact/Booking Details:
☎ **Phone:** +1 808-985-6011
🌐 **Website:** https://www.nps.gov/havo/index.htm

Kilauea Caldera: Lava Flows & Glowing Crater

Visiting Hawai'i Island - also known as the Big Island - is like stepping back in time and forwards into the raw existence of Earth. Never has this been more literal than in the depth of Hawaii Volcanoes National Park (HVNP) and the Kilauea Caldera, the central point of activity for the national park. This park is unique in many ways and worth days of exploration not only for its beauty but also its historical significance and its geology.

Though visitable 287 days a year (or 79% of the calendar year), the Kilauea Volcano itself serves as a beacon to the island from the south side. Vents as recent as 2018 have pitted farmland and eaten away at landmarks as cliffs have been created or pushed back inland. In the evening, plumes of vapors and fumes may be all you see. As the evening grows, a red or pink glow will become increasingly easier to see, until you can't help but linger at the edge of the caldera. Watching the slow but intense rivers of lava will lull you into contemplation of how small and inconsequential our works and worries truly are.

The lava shifts back and forth; forever changing the shape of the island in a matter of years at a rate we are not used to contemplating. Only the relieved hiss of steam marks the flows' passing. In the center of it all, the Halema'uma'u Crater's walls glow brighter as night darkens. In its center, spatter and lava pool in an arcane and fitting measurement of time's passage in the brittle islands.

Thurston Lava Tube: Walking Through Volcanic History

The first visit back in the car, just a few minutes down the road, is to the Thurston Lava Tube, where Ms. Kona told students that walking inside a lava tube is like "walking through a cave, but what we were actually walking through is a material that came from a volcano," she said. Protruding calcium carbonate droplets and countless root-like lava formations gave the cave-like space a distinct look, and Ms. Kona pointed out how, in certain places, striations on the inside of the cave wall could be seen where, millennia ago, there would have been the occasional flood of molten lava deciding the landscape.

Chain of Craters Road: Scenic Drive to the Sea

Following the eruption's progression from the steaming caldera to the active lava delta in 2018 was as simple as driving east on Crater Rim Drive and then descending about 3,700 feet in 20 miles to the sea on Chain of Craters Road. This is one of the most scenic drives in Hawaii. From the crater rim, the road travels through forest to anotherworldly landscape of lava flows ranging from centuries-old blackened rivers of pahoehoe to recent puffy 'a'a'. It parallels Mauna Ulu's dramatic pahoehoe flows before traversing the deep fault in Makaopuhi Crater, north of which you can look down on the strange symmetrical pu'u of the Pauahi Scenic Lookout, or up on the seldom-visited 5-mile pahoehoe flow that created it. When the road reaches the coast, you'll find more craters, tubes, and skylights made accessible by no less than 10 short (1-6 mile round trip) hikes, including Kealakomo Overlook (.7 miles); Hilina Pali Road, which ventures along the rim into an ancient koa forest; and the Po'o Vent, 3 miles one-way, where in 2003 a silvery lava delta poured from the end of an unreported tube. If lava is flowing, it will be on display at the Park's end. Near the coast, as the hardened lava flows steepen into the ocean, cliff-top lookouts face south towards Ka'u. 3 miles past the scenic overlook, the lava covers the road. A stiff breeze lifts the immense, gauzy acres of the Harman'e Pali, which formed from the 1969-1974 eruption of Mauna Ulu.

At the coast something else happens to the pahoehoe. You can see where when you look down from the road at Kealakomo Overlook. The pahoehoe lavas, which all upcountry ignore substantial "chaff" of blocky blue-black and brown to gray cinder-like rock debris. Geologists call it 'a'a'. Everywhere you look from this 1974 break in Chain of Craters Road, 19 miles from the Kilauea Visitor Center, the ropy pahoehoe rolls across the 'a'a' like lava rising in loaf pans, a sight you can explore by walking northwest from the Kealakomo Overlook. It will be several years of small ooze-ups and garden-variety damage before lava once again crosses Chain of Craters Road.

Jaggar Museum: Learning About Volcanic Activity

Located in the center of the Pacific Ocean, the Hawaiian Islands are surrounded in every direction by miles of blue water. Volcanoes have been churning beneath the ocean surface for millions of years, and today, the archipelago is dotted with immense dormant and active cones. Humans have a natural instinct to live as close as possible to the extraordinary features of the world and have been living on these islands since at least 600 AD. Telescopes and other astronomical observatories are noteworthy highlights of Mauna Kea, but the third subtle visitor center on our agenda today is the Thomas A. Jaggar Museum.

The name of the museum represents our next stop. Thomas Jaggar came to Hawaii in 1909 from Harvard and helped start the Hawaiian Volcano Observatory.

In 1912, the scientist established the Volcano Research Center and lived and worked in Kīlauea Crater. Today, he is credited with not only significant advances in the scientific understanding of Hawaiian volcanic processes but is also remembered for bringing the community into the work of the observatory. Although the intensity of volcanic activity waxes and wanes, Kīlauea volcano remains an explosive - active - today. At the entrance to Hawaii Volcanoes National Park, travelers are greeted by an educational sign highlighting different eruptive features and flows.

Learning is part and parcel of travel, and the Jaggar Museum - part of the National Park system - is a great resource. Learn about the ongoing research, as well as the living culture of the indigenous people and how the volcanic geology of the island of Hawaii has changed over the years. Even if you travel without a plan, the landscape's ever-changing beauty provides an amazing snapshot of our world and the place we call home.

Kona Coast: Sun, Sea, & Coffee

Kona Coffee Farms: Tours & Tastings

World-renowned Kona Coffee is grown in the rich, volcanic soil in the shadow of Maunaloa here on the Big Island, and there are over 650 purveyors of the globe's most precious and expensive coffee in these parts. The Historic Kona Coffee Region is on the slopes of Hualalai, the 8th in our chain of 5 mountains. Kona Coffee Country is also known as the North and South Kona Districts, but we islanders simply say, "I live on the mountain," and we're either a mountain person to the north, or to the south. Over 8,000 acres of coffee are cultivated, from the Kohala district to the north of Kona, and the Kona district, all the way to the farmland above Papa Bay in Ka'u, the first district to the south of here.

If you've never seen coffee being produced, cultivated, and dry-processed, the Kona coffee farms are a great educational experience. This prestigious bean got its start in Kona with Reverend Samuel Ruggles in 1828, and it's grown to become the U.S.A. coffee to competitions like Coffee of The Year, red carpeted at places like the Oscars, and sipped by the king and queens of antiquity and the upper echelon all over the world. Many of the Kona Coffee Farms are along the whole humorous and historic Mamalahoa Highway, and have been family owned for generations. Each farm has a distinct style of producing coffee, and almost all of them also give tours of their lands and their mechanical equipment, not just a tasting or coffee cart, so you still learn something of how the coffee is traditionally produced in our land of fire and ice. Some farms are mechanized, but many still use the pulper that drops the beans into wet beds to ferment, and then into dryers on shiny decks of concrete in the sunshine. The processed beans then go through the coffee grader and sorters, are roasted and tasted, for the ultimate money shot at the end of the coffee segment of the visit.

1 Kona Coffee Living History Farm
Description:
Kona Coffee Living History Farm, located in Captain Cook, is the only living history coffee farm in the United States. It offers a glimpse into the lives of early 20th-century Japanese immigrants who pioneered Kona's coffee industry. Visitors can explore the historic farm and learn about traditional coffee cultivation methods.

Location: 82-6199 Mamalahoa Highway, Captain Cook, HI 96704

Getting There:
By Car: Approximately 30 minutes from Kailua-Kona via Highway 11.

Opening Time: Tuesday and Friday, 10:00 AM - 2:00 PM

Prices:
- Adults: $20
- Students (7-17): $10
- Hawaii Residents: $15 (Adults), $5 (Students)

Things to Do:
- Self-Guided Tours: Explore the coffee orchard and historic farmhouse.
- Living History: Interact with costumed interpreters demonstrating traditional crafts and agricultural activities.
- Coffee Tasting: Sample 100% Kona coffee.

Contact/Booking Details:
☎ **Phone:** +1 808-323-3222
🌐 **Website:** https://www.konahistorical.org

2 Greenwell Farms
📑 **Description:**
Greenwell Farms, established in 1850, is one of the oldest coffee farms in Kona. It offers tours that provide insight into coffee cultivation and processing, from bean to cup.

📍 **Location:** 81-6581 Mamalahoa Highway, Kealakekua, HI 96750

🚌 **Getting There:**
By Car: Approximately 25 minutes from Kailua-Kona via Highway 11.

⏰ **Opening Time:** Daily, 9:00 AM - 3:00 PM

💳 **Prices:** Free tours

Things to Do:
- Farm Tours: Learn about the history and process of coffee production.
- Coffee Tasting: Sample various Greenwell Farms coffee blends.
- Shopping: Purchase coffee and local products at the farm store.

Contact/Booking Details:
☎ **Phone:** +1 808-323-2295
🌐 **Website:** https://www.greenwellfarms.com

3 Mountain Thunder Coffee Plantation

📄 **Description:**

Mountain Thunder Coffee Plantation offers tours of its organic coffee farm, located high in the Kona mountains. The tours include coffee tasting and a look at the processing facilities.

🔨 **Location:** 73-1942 Ha'o Street, Kailua-Kona, HI 96740

🚗 **Getting There:**

By Car: Approximately 20 minutes from Kailua-Kona via Kaloko Drive.

⏰ **Opening Time:** Daily, 9:00 AM - 4:00 PM

💳 **Prices:** Free tours

Things to Do:

➡ Farm Tours: Explore the coffee fields and processing facilities.
➡ Coffee Tasting: Enjoy samples of organic Kona coffee.
➡ Nature Walks: Discover the lush surroundings of the plantation.

Contact/Booking Details:

☎ **Phone:** +1 808-325-5566
🌐 **Website:** https://www.mountainthunder.com

4 Kealakekua Bay

📄 **Description:**

Kealakekua Bay is a marine life conservation district known for its clear waters and diverse marine life, making it a top spot for snorkeling and kayaking. The bay is also historically significant as the site where Captain James Cook first landed in Hawaii.

🔨 **Location:** Kealakekua, HI 96750

🚗 **Getting There:**

By Car: Approximately 30 minutes from Kailua-Kona via Highway 11.

⏰ **Opening Time:** Always open

💳 **Prices:** Free entry

Things to Do:
- Snorkeling: Explore the vibrant coral reefs and marine life.
- Kayaking: Paddle across the bay for a closer look at the Captain Cook Monument.
- Hiking: Take a hike to the monument for historical insights.

Contact/Booking Details:
🌐 **Website:** https://www.gohawaii.com

---

5 **Hulihe'e Palace**
📄 **Description:**
Hulihe'e Palace, built in 1838, was the summer residence of Hawaiian royalty. The palace now serves as a museum showcasing Victorian artifacts from the era of King Kalākaua and Queen Kapi'olani.

📍 **Location:** 75-5718 Ali'i Drive, Kailua-Kona, HI 96740

🚗 **Getting There:**
By Car: Located in downtown Kailua-Kona.
⏰ **Opening Time:** Tuesday - Saturday, 10:00 AM - 3:00 PM

💳 **Prices:**
- Adults: $10
- Seniors (60+): $8
- Students (13-17): $1
- Children (under 12): Free

Things to Do:
- Museum Tour: Explore the historic rooms and artifacts.
- Cultural Events: Attend events like hula performances and historical reenactments.

Contact/Booking Details:
☎ **Phone:** +1 808-329-1877
🌐 **Website:** https://daughtersofhawaii.org

⑥ Mokuaikaua Church
📑 **Description:**
Mokuaikaua Church, established in 1820, is the oldest Christian church in Hawaii. The church's historic architecture and beautiful interior make it a notable landmark in Kailua-Kona.

📍 **Location:** 75-5713 Ali'i Drive, Kailua-Kona, HI 96740

🚗 **Getting There:**
By Car: Located in downtown Kailua-Kona.

⏰ **Opening Time:** Daily, 10:00 AM - 2:00 PM

💳 **Prices:** Free entry (donations appreciated)

Things to Do:
➡ Historical Tour: Learn about the church's history and significance.
➡ Architectural Viewing: Admire the beautiful wooden interior and original furnishings.

Contact/Booking Details:
☎ **Phone:** +1 808-329-0655
🌐 **Website:** https://mokuaikaua.org

⑦ Kailua Pier
📑 **Description:**
Kailua Pier is a central hub in Kailua-Kona, known for its bustling activity and scenic views. It's a popular spot for fishing, boat tours, and watching sunsets.

📍 **Location:** 75-5660 Palani Road, Kailua-Kona, HI 96740

🚗 Getting There:
By Car: Located in downtown Kailua-Kona.

⏰ Opening Time: Always open

💳 Prices: Free to visit

Things to Do:
- ➡ Fishing: Cast a line off the pier.
- ➡ Boat Tours: Take a boat tour for snorkeling or dolphin watching.
- ➡ Sunset Viewing: Enjoy beautiful sunsets over the ocean.

Contact/Booking Details:
🌐 **Website:** https://www.gohawaii.com

---

8 Pu'uhonua o Hōnaunau National Historical Park
📄 Description:
Pu'uhonua o Hōnaunau National Historical Park preserves a sacred Hawaiian refuge. The park includes royal grounds and structures like the Great Wall and Hale o Keawe temple, offering insights into ancient Hawaiian culture.

📍 Location: 1871 Trail, Hōnaunau, HI 96726

🚗 Getting There:
By Car: Approximately 40 minutes from Kailua-Kona via Highway 11.

⏰ Opening Time: Daily, 7:00 AM - 8:00 PM

💳 Prices:
- ➡ Private vehicle: $20
- ➡ Motorcycle: $15
- ➡ Individual pedestrian/bicycle: $10

Things to Do:
➡ Historical Exploration: Tour the royal grounds and sacred sites.
➡ Cultural Programs: Attend demonstrations and cultural talks.

Contact/Booking Details:
☎ **Phone:** +1 808-328-2326
🌐 **Website:** https://www.nps.gov/puho/index.htm

9 Kahaluʻu Beach Park
📄 **Description:**
Kahaluʻu Beach Park, also known as "Turtle Beach," is famous for its excellent snorkeling conditions and abundant marine life, including green sea turtles.

🗺 **Location:** Ali'i Drive, Kailua-Kona, HI 96740

🚌 **Getting There:**
By Car: About 10 minutes from downtown Kailua-Kona.
⏰ **Opening Time:** Always open

💳 **Prices:** Free to visit

Things to Do:
➡ Snorkeling: Explore the coral reefs and observe marine life.
➡ Turtle Watching: Spot green sea turtles along the shore.

Contact/Booking Details:
🌐 **Website:** https://www.gohawaii.com

10 Magic Sands Beach Park
📄 **Description:**
Magic Sands Beach Park, also known as Laʻaloa Beach, is famous for its white sand that disappears and reappears seasonally, influenced by high surf. This dynamic beach is popular for swimming, boogie boarding, and sunbathing.

✎ **Location:** 77-6452 Ali'i Drive, Kailua-Kona, HI 96740

🚗 **Getting There:**
By Car: About 10 minutes from downtown Kailua-Kona.
⏰ **Opening Time:** Always open

💳 **Prices:** Free to visit

Things to Do:
➡ Swimming and Boogie Boarding: Enjoy the waves, especially during the summer months.
➡ Sunbathing: Relax on the sandy beach.
➡ Picnicking: Utilize the picnic tables and barbecue grills available.

Contact/Booking Details:
🌐 **Website:** https://www.gohawaii.com

Hilo Side: Waterfalls, Rainforests, & Culture

The big draw in this part of the island is, of course, the Hawaii Volcanoes National Park. The park's centerpiece is the active Kilauea Volcano. Most of the attractions and activities revolve around the volcano or its offshoot, the still-flowing Puu Oo vent. Within the park, consider hiking the Crater Rim Trail, which circles Kilauea. The vent itself can be reached via driving, though it is open to the public only for a short period of time during their visitor minutes given the eruptive activity. For a detour, turn off the Crater Rim Road to Devastation Trail. Then continue on the Crater Rim Road to the Thurston Lava Tube. Further down the road are the Sulfur Banks, and eventually the Steam Vents.

A number of important natural attractions are clustered on the Hilo side of the island, where the terrain is wet and varied. The Hawaii Volcanoes National Park is located here. You will also find the Lava Tree State Park, where a gentler eruption from the early 20th century created some impressive sights. More rock formations and lava tubes can be seen at the Kaumana Caves Park, and then you get to experience a unique ecosystem as you follow the trail of the Pu'u O'o Trail. Make a stop at the Kaola Farm, a sprawling contract flower farm, and finally visit Puna District Center. A golf course and a black sand beach await you there.

In contrast to the hot and dry southwest side of the Big Island are the much cooler, moist slopes in the northwest. Annual rainfall levels on the island range from nearly zero to 35 feet, but the average throughout the island state doesn't exceed 18 inches per year. Wild pigs signal their presence in this area and on all parts of the island with root-field circles that closely resemble patterns formed when a bellicose, worn, shirtless, pattern-bald male police officer stands with legs slightly spread as he orders by word, conversational (recorded, as well as news), whether or not be recorded and whisper the accomplice, where he expects disposable evidence to materialize. It litters the island's ditches, among volcanic axes that last violently erupted when the dinosaurs roamed the earth, forming a thin soil over the work debris and ancient dam structure cells remains once harvested, protected, and so delightfully displayed here.

Imagine an island so geologically young that the organisms and looks of its living rocks and stone fields, bare of soils or vegetative covers, are hundreds of years old rather than millennia, a speck of life emerged from cosmic mists in your own lifetime rather than in ancient times. The geologic youth is in part due to the diversity of lava flows - Pahoehoe, aa, block rubble, and the highly dangerous but little known blocks-toed type of flow. Only 50 centuries or so ago, Mauna Loa, one of five volcanic mountains on the Big Island of Hawaii, was still a bare lava rock hill not too much unlike the one photographed. In 1983, a walk across the brilliantly orange and yellow side-to-side-spreading toes of the lava in a volcanic vegetative zone resembled walking through a star's arms as it reaches for the infinite.

1 Akaka Falls State Park
📑 Description:
Akaka Falls State Park, located on the northeastern side of Hawaii's Big Island, features a stunning 442-foot waterfall surrounded by lush tropical rainforest. Visitors can enjoy a short, paved loop trail that offers views of both Akaka Falls and the nearby Kahuna Falls. The park is a haven for nature lovers, with its vibrant orchids, bamboo groves, and diverse ferns.

📍 **Location:** 875 Akaka Falls Road, Honomu, HI 96728

🚗 **Getting There:**
By Car: From Hilo, head north on Highway 19 for about 11 miles. Turn right onto Akaka Falls Road (Highway 220) and follow it for approximately 3.5 miles to the park entrance.

⏰ **Opening Time:** Daily from 8:30 AM to 5:00 PM

🟰 **Prices:**
- ➡ Entry Fee: $5.00 per person for non-residents (children under 3 are free)
- ➡ Parking Fee: $10.00 per vehicle for non-residents
- ➡ Hawaii residents enter and park for free with a valid Hawaii ID

Things to Do:

➡ Hiking: Enjoy a scenic 0.4-mile loop trail through the rainforest.

➡ Sightseeing: Take in the breathtaking views of Akaka Falls and Kahuna Falls.

➡ Photography: Capture the beauty of the waterfalls and the lush tropical environment.

➡ Wildlife Observation: Spot native bird species and the unique o'opu 'alamo'o fish.

Contact/Booking Details:

☎ **Phone:** +1 808-974-6200

🌐 **Website:** www.hawaiistateparks.org/parks/akaka-falls-state-park

2 Rainbow Falls

📑 **Description:**

Rainbow Falls, also known as Waiānuenue, is an 80-foot waterfall located in Wailuku River State Park near downtown Hilo. The falls are named for the rainbows that appear in the mist during sunny mornings. The broad waterfall plunges over a natural lava cave into the river below, offering a stunning display of natural beauty. The area is lush with tropical flora, making it a picturesque spot for visitors.

📐 **Location:** 967 Waianuenue Avenue, Hilo, HI 96720

🚗 **Getting There:**

By Car: From downtown Hilo, head north on Waianuenue Avenue for about one mile. Turn left onto Rainbow Drive and follow the signs to the park entrance.

⏰ **Opening Time:** Daily from 7:00 AM to 5:30 PM

💳 **Prices:** Free entry

Things to Do:

➡ Hiking: Explore the Rainbow Falls Trail, a short and easy hike that offers spectacular views of the falls.

➡ Photography: Capture the stunning rainbows that often form in the mist of the falls in the early morning light.

➡ Picnicking: Enjoy a picnic in the designated area with lush greenery and views of the waterfall.

➡ Nearby Attractions: Visit Pe'epe'e Falls and the Boiling Pots located further upstream in Wailuku River State Park.

Contact/Booking Details:

⊕ **Website:** www.gohawaii.com

③ Boiling Pots

📑 **Description:**

Boiling Pots are terraced pools along the Wailuku River, known for their bubbling appearance caused by the rapid water flow over the basalt lava rock formations. The site is part of Wailuku River State Park and offers a unique and dramatic natural landscape.

🔨 **Location:** Pe'epe'e Falls Drive, Hilo, HI 96720

🚙 **Getting There:**

By Car: From downtown Hilo, take Waianuenue Avenue west and follow signs to the Boiling Pots parking area.

⏰ **Opening Time:** Daily from 9:00 AM to 6:00 PM

💳 **Prices:** Free entry

Things to Do:

➡ Sightseeing: View the dramatic boiling effect of the water in the terraced pools.

➡ Hiking: Explore the trails leading to various viewpoints of the Boiling Pots and Pe'epe'e Falls.

➡ Photography: Capture the unique landscape and water flow, especially during the wet season.

Contact/Booking Details:
🌐 Website: www.hawaii-guide.com

4 Hawaii Tropical Botanical Garden
📑 **Description:**
The Hawaii Tropical Botanical Garden is a 40-acre valley with over 2,000 species of tropical plants. It offers a tranquil escape with scenic trails, water features, and vibrant plant life.

🔨 **Location:** 27-717 Old Mamalahoa Highway, Papaikou, HI 96781

🚠 **Getting There:**
By Car: About 8.5 miles north of Hilo on Highway 19, turn right onto Old Mamalahoa Highway and follow signs to the garden.

⏰ **Opening Time:** Daily from 9:00 AM to 5:00 PM

💳 **Prices:**
- Adults: $20
- Children (6-16): $5
- Children under 6: Free

Things to Do:
- Self-**Guided Tours:** Wander through the lush gardens and enjoy the diverse plant species.
- Photography: Capture the beauty of the tropical flora and the picturesque ocean views.
- Educational Displays: Learn about the various plants and their ecological significance.

Contact/Booking Details:
☎ **Phone:** +1 808-964-5233
🌐 **Website:** www.htbg.com

5 Lili'uokalani Gardens
📄 **Description:**
Lili'uokalani Gardens is a serene, 24-acre Japanese garden located in Hilo, named after Queen Lili'uokalani. The garden features koi ponds, pagodas, stone lanterns, and a teahouse, reflecting traditional Japanese landscaping.

📍 **Location:** 189 Lihiwai Street, Hilo, HI 96720

🚘 **Getting There:**
By Car: From downtown Hilo, head east on Banyan Drive and turn right onto Lihiwai Street.

⏰ **Opening Time:** Open 24 hours daily

💳 **Prices:** Free entry

Things to Do:
- Walking: Stroll through the beautifully landscaped gardens.
- Photography: Capture the serene beauty of the garden's traditional Japanese features.
- Picnicking: Enjoy a peaceful picnic by the koi ponds and bridges.

Contact/Booking Details:
🌐 **Website:** www.gohawaii.com

6 Pacific Tsunami Museum
📄 **Description:**
The Pacific Tsunami Museum in Hilo educates visitors about tsunamis and their impact on the Pacific region. The museum features exhibits on the history, science, and personal stories related to tsunamis.

📍 **Location:** 130 Kamehameha Avenue, Hilo, HI 96720

🚘 **Getting There:**
By Car: Located in downtown Hilo on Kamehameha Avenue.

⏰ **Opening Time:** Tuesday to Saturday, 10:00 AM to 4:00 PM

💳 **Prices:**
- Adults: $8
- Seniors (60+): $7
- Students: $4
- Children under 6: Free

Things to Do:
- Exhibits: Explore interactive displays and historical exhibits about tsunamis.
- Educational Programs: Participate in educational programs and guided tours.
- Gift Shop: Browse tsunami-related books, souvenirs, and educational materials.

Contact/Booking Details:
☎ **Phone:** +1 808-935-0926
🌐 **Website:** www.tsunami.org

[7] **Lyman Museum & Mission House**
📑 **Description:**
The Lyman Museum & Mission House in Hilo showcases the natural and cultural history of Hawaii. The museum includes exhibits on Hawaiian culture, geology, and a historic mission house built in 1839.

📍 **Location:** 276 Haili Street, Hilo, HI 96720

🚗 **Getting There:**
By Car: Located in downtown Hilo, accessible via Kinoole Street.

⏰ **Opening Time:** Monday to Saturday, 10:00 AM to 4:30 PM

Prices:
- Adults: $10
- Seniors (60+): $8
- Children (6-17): $3
- Children under 6: Free

Things to Do:
- Exhibits: Explore cultural and natural history exhibits.
- Mission House Tour: Take a guided tour of the historic mission house.
- Gift Shop: Purchase unique Hawaiian gifts and educational materials.

Contact/Booking Details:
- **Phone:** +1 808-935-5021
- **Website:** www.lymanmuseum.org

8 Imiloa Astronomy Center
Description:

The Imiloa Astronomy Center in Hilo combines Hawaiian culture and astronomy, offering interactive exhibits, planetarium shows, and educational programs.

Location: 600 Imiloa Place, Hilo, HI 96720

Getting There:

By Car: Located on the University of Hawaii at Hilo campus, accessible via Nowelo Street.

Opening Time: Tuesday to Sunday, 9:00 AM to 5:00 PM

Prices:
- Adults: $19
- Seniors (60+): $16
- Children (5-12): $12
- Children under 5: Free

Things to Do:
- ▶ Planetarium Shows: Enjoy immersive planetarium shows about space and Hawaiian navigation.
- ▶ Interactive Exhibits: Explore exhibits that blend astronomy and Hawaiian culture.
- ▶ Educational Programs: Participate in workshops and educational activities.

Contact/Booking Details:
- ☎ **Phone:** +1 808-932-8901
- 🌐 **Website:** www.imiloahawaii.org

Hamakua Coast: Scenic Drives & Hidden Gems

Craving more of our Hawaiian Zodiac experience, we set our sights on Akaka Falls, a thundering waterfall that could be seen from the protective comfort of a sheltered overlook. As trail-seeking walkers, however, we chose the outer loop trail that wound through the wettest rainforest, an up and down walk that revealed even more lively botanical wonders. Our time, once again, was well spent

The lush Hamakua Coast stretches along the northeastern shore of the Big Island of Hawaii. Set amid great natural beauty, this part of the island is rich in significant Hawaiian history and culture, as well as natural wonders. Maunakea Mountain, with its summit often snow-capped during winter months, and Mauna Loa, hugging Hawaii's only rain forests, tower majestically behind, creating a spectacular backdrop. Nearby to the west, the striking Waipio Valley stretches down to the sea.

Hamakua scenery is marked by Hakalau Gulch, with its steep, densely-forested cliffs and waterfalls, and by rural rolling pastures backed with vistas of mountain forests and ocean. Proprietor-run bed and breakfasts and comfortable inns, some tucked away amid tropical gardens or set amidst working cattle ranches, offer friendly hospitality, picturesque settings, often some of the best ocean views on the island.

Hamakua Coast: Scenic Drives & Hidden Gems

1 Waipio Valley

Description:
Waipio Valley, also known as the "Valley of the Kings," is a stunning and historically significant valley on the northern coast of the Big Island. The valley is about a mile wide and six miles deep, surrounded by cliffs up to 2,000 feet high. It features taro fields, a black sand beach, and several waterfalls, including Hiʻilawe Falls, which is one of the tallest waterfalls in Hawaii.

Location: End of Highway 240, Honokaa, HI 96727

Getting There:
By Car: From Waimea or Hilo, take Highway 19 to Highway 240 and follow it for nearly 10 miles to the Waipio Valley Lookout.

Opening Time: Always open

Prices: Free entry

Things to Do:

➡ Scenic View: Enjoy panoramic views from the Waipio Valley Lookout.

➡ Hiking: Explore trails like the Muliwai Trail for deeper valley views.

➡ Horseback Riding: Take a tour with local stables to explore the valley.

➡ Photography: Capture breathtaking views of the valley and waterfalls.

➡ Black Sand Beach: Relax or walk along the beautiful black sand beach.

Contact/Booking Details:

🌐 **Website:** www.gohawaii.com

2 Waipio Valley Lookout

📑 **Description:**

The Waipio Valley Lookout provides a stunning vantage point to view the lush, green valley, dramatic cliffs, and the black sand beach. The lookout is a popular spot for photography and offers breathtaking views of the valley below.

📍 **Location:** End of Highway 240, Honokaa, HI 96727

🚗 **Getting There:**

By Car: From Waimea or Hilo, take Highway 19 to Highway 240 and follow it for nearly 10 miles to the lookout.

⏰ **Opening Time:** Always open

💳 **Prices:** Free entry

Things to Do:

➡ Photography: Capture the valley's stunning vistas.

➡ Picnicking: Enjoy a meal with a view at the picnic area.

➡ Relaxing: Simply take in the beauty of the valley from above.

Contact/Booking Details:
⊕ **Website:** www.gohawaii.com

---

3 **Hiʻilawe Falls (view from a distance)**

📄 **Description:**

Hiʻilawe Falls is one of the tallest waterfalls in Hawaii, plunging approximately 1,450 feet down the cliffs at the back of Waipio Valley. The falls can be viewed from a distance within the valley.

📍 **Location:** Waipio Valley, HI 96727

🚘 **Getting There:**

By Car: Follow directions to Waipio Valley Lookout and hike or take a tour into the valley.

⏰ **Opening Time:** Always open

💳 **Prices:** Free entry

Things to Do:

➡ Sightseeing: View the majestic falls from various points in the valley.
➡ Photography: Capture the falls from the valley floor or on a hike.

Contact/Booking Details:
⊕ **Website:** www.hawaii-guide.com

---

4 **Laupāhoehoe Point Beach Park**

📄 **Description:**

Laupāhoehoe Point Beach Park is a scenic park on the Hamakua Coast known for its rugged coastline, tide pools, and powerful waves. It offers a serene environment with beautiful ocean views and a memorial for those lost in the 1946 tsunami.

📍 **Location:** Laupahoehoe Point Road, Laupahoehoe, HI 96764

Getting There:
By Car: From Hilo, take Highway 19 north to Laupahoehoe Point Road.

Opening Time: Always open

Prices: Free entry

Things to Do:
- Picnicking: Use the picnic areas and pavilions for a meal.
- Exploring: Wander along the rocky shoreline and tide pools.
- Memorial: Visit the tsunami memorial site.

Contact/Booking Details:
- Website: www.gohawaii.com

5 Kolekole Beach Park
Description:
Kolekole Beach Park is a small, picturesque park along the Hamakua Coast. The park is located at the mouth of the Kolekole Stream, offering a scenic spot with picnic areas, a swimming hole, and lush surroundings.

Location: Highway 19, Honomu, HI 96728

Getting There:
By Car: Located just off Highway 19, near the 14-mile marker north of Hilo.

Opening Time: Always open

Prices: Free entry

Things to Do:
- Swimming: Enjoy the natural swimming hole at the park.
- Picnicking: Use the picnic facilities for a relaxing meal.

◉ Sightseeing: Take in the lush surroundings and scenic views.

Contact/Booking Details:

⊕ Website: www.hawaii-guide.com

---

6 **'Akaka Falls State Park (if not visited from Hilo side)**
📄 **Description:**
'Akaka Falls State Park features the stunning 442-foot 'Akaka Falls and the smaller Kahuna Falls. The park is surrounded by lush tropical rainforest and offers a short, scenic loop trail for visitors.

⚒ **Location:** 875 Akaka Falls Road, Honomu, HI 96728

🚗 **Getting There:** By Car: From Hilo, head north on Highway 19 and turn onto Akaka Falls Road.

⏰ **Opening Time:** Daily from 8:30 AM to 5:00 PM

🖶 **Prices:**
◉ Entry Fee: $5.00 per person for non-residents
◉ Parking Fee: $10.00 per vehicle for non-residents

Things to Do:
◉ Hiking: Walk the 0.4-mile loop trail.
◉ Sightseeing: View the impressive 'Akaka Falls and Kahuna Falls.
◉ Photography: Capture the falls and lush surroundings.

Contact/Booking Details:
☎ **Phone:** +1 808-974-6200
⊕ **Website:** www.hawaiistateparks.org

---

7 **Hawaii Tropical Botanical Garden (if not visited from Hilo side)**
📄 **Description:**
The Hawaii Tropical Botanical Garden is a 40-acre valley featuring over 2,000 species of tropical plants. It offers scenic trails, water

features, and vibrant plant life, providing a peaceful escape into nature.

Location: 27-717 Old Mamalahoa Highway, Papaikou, HI 96781

Getting There:
By Car: About 8.5 miles north of Hilo on Highway 19, turn right onto Old Mamalahoa Highway.

Opening Time: Daily from 9:00 AM to 5:00 PM

Prices:
- Adults: $20
- Children (6-16): $5
- Children under 6: Free

Things to Do:
- Self-Guided Tours: Wander through the lush gardens.
- Photography: Capture the tropical flora and ocean views.
- Educational Displays: Learn about the diverse plant species.

Contact/Booking Details:
- **Phone:** +1 808-964-5233
- **Website:** www.htbg.com

CHAPTER 4: ACTIVITIES & ADVENTURES ON OAHU & BIG ISLAND

Water Sports: Surfing, Snorkeling, Diving, Sailing

Oahu and the Big Island offer some of the best water sports experiences in the world, ranging from the iconic surfing spots of Waikiki to the vibrant coral reefs perfect for snorkeling and diving. Whether you are a seasoned water sports enthusiast or a beginner looking to catch your first wave, these islands have something for everyone. Personally, one of my most memorable experiences was snorkeling in Hanauma Bay on Oahu, where I was mesmerized by the colorful fish and intricate coral formations. The thrill of swimming alongside sea turtles and exploring underwater caves left a lasting impression and a deep appreciation for the marine life that thrives in Hawaii's waters.

Top 5 Water Sports Destinations

1 Waikiki Beach, Oahu (Surfing)

📑 Description:

Waikiki Beach is the birthplace of modern surfing and offers gentle waves perfect for beginners and intermediate surfers. The beach is lined with surf schools and rental shops, making it easy to get started.

Location: Honolulu, HI 96815

🚗 Getting There:

- By Car: Located in the heart of Honolulu, accessible via Kalakaua Avenue.
- By Bus: Several bus routes stop near Waikiki Beach.

💳 Prices:

- Surfboard Rental: $10-$20 per hour
- Surf Lessons: $75-$150 for a 1-2 hour lesson

Guided Tours:

- Hans Hedemann Surf School (www.hhsurf.com)
- Waikiki Beach Services (www.waikikibeachservices.com)

2 Hanauma Bay, Oahu (Snorkeling)

📑 Description:

Hanauma Bay is a protected marine life conservation area renowned for its clear waters and abundant marine life, making it an ideal snorkeling spot.

Location: 7455 Kalaniana'ole Highway, Honolulu, HI 96825

🚗 Getting There:
- By Car: About 10 miles east of Waikiki on Kalaniana'ole Highway.
- By Bus: Take Bus Route 22 or 23 from Waikiki.

💳 Prices:
- Entry Fee: $25 per person
- Snorkel Gear Rental: $20 per set

Guided Tours:
Hanauma Bay Snorkel Adventures (www.hanaumabaytours.com)

③ Kona Coast, Big Island (Diving)
📄 Description:
The Kona Coast offers world-class diving sites with clear waters, lava tubes, and vibrant marine life, including the famous manta ray night dives.

📍 Location: Kailua-Kona, HI 96740

🚗 Getting There:
By Car: Accessible via Queen Ka'ahumanu Highway (Hwy 19).

💳 Prices:
- Dive Trips: $150-$200 per dive
- Equipment Rental: $50-$75 per day

Guided Tours:
- Kona Honu Divers (www.konahonudivers.com)
- Jack's Diving Locker (www.jacksdivinglocker.com)

④ Kealakekua Bay, Big Island (Snorkeling)
📄 Description:
Kealakekua Bay is a marine sanctuary known for its pristine waters, coral reefs, and historical significance as the site where Captain Cook first landed in Hawaii.

📍 **Location:** Kealakekua, HI 96750

🚕 **Getting There:**
➡ By Car: About 12 miles south of Kailua-Kona via Highway 11.
➡ By Boat: Several tour operators provide boat access to the bay.

💳 **Prices:**
➡ Snorkel Gear Rental: $20 per set
➡ Kayak Rental: $50-$75 per day

Guided Tours:
➡ Kona Boys (www.konaboys.com)
➡ Fair Wind Cruises (www.fair-wind.com)

5 North Shore, Oahu (Surfing)
📄 **Description:**
The North Shore of Oahu is famous for its big wave surfing during the winter months and offers some of the best waves in the world for experienced surfers.

📍 **Location:** Haleiwa, HI 96712

🚕 **Getting There:**
By Car: About 30 miles north of Honolulu via H-2 and Kamehameha Highway.

💳 **Prices:**
➡ Surfboard Rental: $15-$25 per hour
➡ Surf Lessons: $100-$200 for a 2-hour lesson

Guided Tours:
➡ North Shore Surf Girls (www.northshoresurfgirls.com)
➡ Sunset Suzy's Surf School (www.sunsetsuzy.com)

These top water sports destinations on Oahu and the Big Island offer a variety of activities for all skill levels. Whether you're looking to ride the waves, explore the underwater world, or sail the open seas, Hawaii's waters are sure to provide unforgettable adventures.

Land Adventures: Hiking, Ziplining, ATV Tours, Helicopter Tours

Oahu and the Big Island are not only renowned for their stunning beaches and water activities but also offer a plethora of land-based adventures. From hiking through lush rainforests and volcanic landscapes to soaring above the islands on a thrilling zipline or helicopter tour, there are countless ways to explore the diverse terrain and natural beauty of Hawaii. I vividly remember my first hike up Diamond Head on Oahu, where the panoramic views of Waikiki and the Pacific Ocean from the summit were simply breathtaking. It's these kinds of experiences that make land adventures in Hawaii truly unforgettable.

Top 5 Land Adventure Destinations

⬚1⬚ Diamond Head State Monument, Oahu (Hiking)

📄 **Description:**

Diamond Head is an iconic volcanic crater offering a moderate hike with rewarding panoramic views of Honolulu and the Pacific Ocean. The trail includes a series of switchbacks and a steep staircase leading to the summit.

📌 **Location:** Diamond Head Road, Honolulu, HI 96815

🚗 **Getting There:**

➡ By Car: Accessible via Diamond Head Road from Waikiki.

➡ By Bus: Take Bus Route 2 or 23 from Waikiki.

💳 **Prices:**

Entry Fee: $5 per car or $1 per pedestrian

Guided Tours:

Hawaii Forest & Trail (www.hawaiiforest.com)

⬚2⬚ Akaka Falls State Park, Big Island (Hiking)

📄 **Description:**

Akaka Falls State Park features a short, scenic hike through lush rainforest to view two majestic waterfalls, Akaka Falls (442 feet) and Kahuna Falls (100 feet).

📌 **Location:** 875 Akaka Falls Road, Honomu, HI 96728

🚗 **Getting There:**

By Car: About 11 miles north of Hilo on Highway 19, turn onto Akaka Falls Road.

💳 **Prices:**

➡ Entry Fee: $5 per person for non-residents

➡ Parking Fee: $10 per vehicle for non-residents

Guided Tours:
Hawaii Forest & Trail (www.hawaiiforest.com)

3 Hilo and Hamakua Coast, Big Island (Ziplining)
📄 **Description:**
Experience the thrill of ziplining over waterfalls, lush valleys, and scenic coastlines on the Hamakua Coast. Several operators offer a variety of zipline tours suitable for all ages and experience levels.

📍 **Location:** Hamakua Coast, HI 96727

🚗 **Getting There:**
By Car: Accessible via Highway 19 north of Hilo.

🚬 **Prices:**
Zipline Tours: $150-$200 per person

Guided Tours:
- Umauma Experience (www.umaumaexperience.com)
- Skyline Eco-Adventures (www.zipline.com)

4 Kualoa Ranch, Oahu (ATV Tours)
📄 **Description:**
Kualoa Ranch offers exciting ATV tours through the scenic valleys and mountains made famous by Hollywood movies. Explore the lush landscapes and discover hidden gems of this historic ranch.

📍 **Location:** 49-560 Kamehameha Highway, Kaneohe, HI 96744

🚗 **Getting There:**
By Car: About 45 minutes from Honolulu via H-1 and Kamehameha Highway.

🚬 **Prices:**
ATV Tours: $130-$160 per person

Guided Tours:
Kualoa Ranch (www.kualoa.com)

5 Volcanoes National Park, Big Island (Helicopter Tours)
📑 Description:
Witness the dramatic landscapes of Volcanoes National Park from the air. Helicopter tours provide breathtaking views of active volcanoes, lava flows, and the diverse terrain of the Big Island.

📍 Location: Volcanoes National Park, HI 96718

🚗 Getting There:
By Car: About 30 miles southwest of Hilo on Highway 11.

💳 Prices:
Helicopter Tours: $250-$400 per person

Guided Tours:
- Blue Hawaiian Helicopters (www.bluehawaiian.com)
- Paradise Helicopters (www.paradisecopters.com)

These top land adventure destinations on Oahu and the Big Island offer a variety of activities for all thrill seekers and nature lovers. Whether you're hiking to breathtaking vistas, zipping through lush valleys, exploring rugged terrain on an ATV, or soaring above volcanic landscapes, Hawaii's land adventures promise unforgettable experiences.

Cultural Experiences: Luaus, Hula Shows, Museums, Festivals

Hawaii is a treasure trove of cultural experiences that provide a deep insight into its rich heritage and traditions. From the mesmerizing hula performances to the immersive luaus, and from historic museums to vibrant festivals, there's something for everyone looking to dive into the Hawaiian culture. One of my favorite cultural experiences was attending the Merrie Monarch Hula Festival in Hilo. The grace and storytelling through hula left a lasting impression, showcasing the profound connection Hawaiians have with their history and environment.

Top 5 Cultural Experience Destinations

[1] **Polynesian Cultural Center, Oahu**

📑 **Description:**

The Polynesian Cultural Center is a unique theme park that offers an immersive experience into the cultures of Polynesia. It features six island villages, each representing different Polynesian cultures, with live demonstrations, interactive exhibits, and a grand luau and evening show.

📍 **Location:** 55-370 Kamehameha Highway, Laie, HI 96762

🚗 **Getting There:**
- By Car: Approximately one hour from Honolulu via H-1 and Kamehameha Highway.
- By Bus: Take Bus Route 60 from Waikiki.

💳 **Prices:**
- General Admission: $69.95
- Packages (including luau and evening show): $139.95-$219.95

Best Time to Visit: Open daily except Sundays, 12:00 PM - 9:00 PM

Guided Tours:
Polynesian Cultural Center (www.polynesia.com)

② **Bishop Museum, Oahu**
📄 **Description:**
The Bishop Museum is Hawaii's premier natural and cultural history museum, showcasing artifacts and exhibits on the history of Hawaii and the Pacific. It provides insights into Polynesian migration, the Hawaiian monarchy, and local flora and fauna.

📍 **Location:** 1525 Bernice Street, Honolulu, HI 96817

🚗 **Getting There:**
- By Car: Accessible via H-1 Freeway.
- By Bus: Several bus routes stop near the museum.

💳 **Prices:**
- Adults: $24.95
- Children (4-17): $16.95

Best Time to Visit: Open daily, 9:00 AM - 5:00 PM

Guided Tours:
Bishop Museum (www.bishopmuseum.org)

③ Waimea Valley, Oahu
📑 **Description:**
Waimea Valley offers a blend of cultural and natural attractions, including botanical gardens and historic sites. Visitors can learn about Hawaiian history and culture through various exhibits and take a refreshing dip in the waterfall at the end of the valley.

📍 **Location:** 59-864 Kamehameha Highway, Haleiwa, HI 96712

🚌 **Getting There:**
By Car: Located on the North Shore, accessible via H-2 and Kamehameha Highway.

🎫 **Prices:**
➡ General Admission: $20
➡ Children (4-12): $12

Best Time to Visit: Open daily, 9:00 AM - 5:00 PM

Guided Tours:
Waimea Valley (www.waimeavalley.net)

④ Merrie Monarch Hula Festival, Big Island
📑 **Description:**
The Merrie Monarch Hula Festival is an annual week-long cultural event dedicated to the art of hula. It features hula competitions, cultural demonstrations, and a grand parade, celebrating the rich heritage of Hawaiian dance.

📍 **Location:** Hilo, HI 96720

Getting There:
- By Car: Various locations in Hilo.
- By Bus: Local transit options available in Hilo.

Prices:
Event tickets: Prices vary by event, book early as they sell out quickly.

Best Time to Visit: Held annually during the week after Easter

Guided Tours:
Merrie Monarch Festival (www.merriemonarch.com)

---

5 Pu'uhonua o Hōnaunau National Historical Park, Big Island
Description:
This sacred site, also known as the Place of Refuge, was historically a sanctuary for those who broke ancient Hawaiian laws. Today, it offers visitors a glimpse into traditional Hawaiian life and the historical significance of the area.

Location: 1871 Trail, Honaunau, HI 96726

Getting There:
By Car: About 20 miles south of Kailua-Kona via Highway 11.

Prices:
Entrance Fee: $10 per vehicle

Best Time to Visit: Open daily, 7:00 AM - sunset

Guided Tours:
Pu'uhonua o Hōnaunau National Historical Park
(www.nps.gov/puho)

These top cultural destinations provide a deep dive into the history and traditions of Hawaii, offering a mix of educational and immersive experiences. Whether attending a vibrant festival, exploring a historic park, or enjoying a traditional luau, these experiences highlight the unique cultural heritage of Oahu and the Big Island.

Culinary Delights: Food Tours, Farmers Markets, Cooking Classes

Hawaii's culinary scene is a vibrant mix of traditional Hawaiian cuisine, local farm-to-table dishes, and innovative flavors. Exploring the food culture here offers a delicious insight into the islands' rich heritage. I remember my first visit to a farmers market in Kailua, where the fresh tropical fruits, local delicacies, and friendly vendors made me feel truly connected to the island's community. Here are the top culinary experiences you shouldn't miss on Oahu and the Big Island.

Top 5 Culinary Experience Destinations

1 Honolulu Food Tour: Eat Like a Local, Oahu

📄 Description:

This food tour takes you through Honolulu's diverse culinary scene, offering tastings from local favorites and hidden gems. You'll sample dishes like poke, malasadas, and plate lunches while learning about the island's food culture.

📍 Location: Various locations in Honolulu, HI

🚘 Getting There:
- ➡ By Car: Accessible via main roads in Honolulu.
- ➡ By Bus: Multiple bus routes available in Honolulu.

💳 Prices: $150 per person

Pros and Cons:
Pros: Diverse food tastings, knowledgeable guides, immersive experience
Cons: Pricey, limited to Honolulu area

Guided Tours:
🌐 Website: www.alohafoodtours.com

2 Waikiki Farmers Market, Oahu

📄 Description:

Located inside the Hyatt Regency, this farmers market offers a variety of fresh local produce, prepared foods, and artisanal products. It's a great spot for a quick bite or to pick up unique souvenirs.

📍 Location: 2424 Kalakaua Ave, Honolulu, HI 96815

🚘 Getting There:
- ➡ By Car: Parking available at the Hyatt Regency.
- ➡ By Bus: Several bus routes stop near Waikiki.

Prices:
- Entry: Free
- Food items: $5-$15

Pros and Cons:
- **Pros:** Wide variety of fresh and local products, convenient location
- **Cons:** Can be crowded, higher prices due to tourist area

Guided Tours: Not applicable

③ Farm to Table Cooking Class at Kulaniapia Falls, Big Island
Description:
This cooking class offers a hands-on experience where you harvest ingredients from the farm and prepare a meal while enjoying stunning views of Kulaniapia Falls.

Location: 100 Kulaniapia Drive, Hilo, HI 96720

Getting There:
By Car: Located near Hilo, accessible via local roads.

Prices: $169 per person

Pros and Cons:
Pros: Fresh ingredients, beautiful setting, educational
Cons: Weather dependent, limited class sizes

Guided Tours:
- **Website:** www.viator.com

④ Hamakua Harvest Farmers Market, Big Island
Description:
Held every Sunday, this farmers market features local produce, handmade goods, and live entertainment. It's a community-focused event where you can taste the flavors of the Big Island.

📍 **Location:** 44-2600 Mamalahoa Highway, Honokaa, HI 96727

🚕 **Getting There:**
By Car: Accessible via Highway 19.

💳 **Prices:**
➡ Entry: Free
➡ Food items: $3-$20

Pros and Cons:
Pros: Fresh, local produce, family-friendly, live music
Cons: Only open on Sundays, can be crowded

Guided Tours: Not applicable

5 Hawaiian-Style Cooking Class, Oahu
📄 **Description:**
This hands-on cooking class focuses on traditional Hawaiian dishes using local ingredients. You'll learn to make dishes like poke, lau lau, and haupia, and enjoy a meal at the end.

📍 **Location:** Various locations in Honolulu, HI

🚕 **Getting There:**
➡ By Car: Locations vary, check website for details.
➡ By Bus: Multiple bus routes available in Honolulu.

💳 **Prices:** $125 per person

Pros and Cons:
Pros: Authentic Hawaiian recipes, interactive experience, small class sizes
Cons: Locations can vary, limited availability

Guided Tours:
🌐 **Website:** www.hawaiianstylecookingclass.com

CHAPTER 6: PRACTICAL INFORMATION FOR OAHU & BIG ISLAND

Visas & Entry Requirements

Hawaii, as a U.S. state, has specific entry requirements that vary depending on your nationality and the purpose of your visit.

U.S. Citizens:
No visa is required for U.S. citizens to travel to Hawaii. A valid government-issued photo ID (like a driver's license) is sufficient for domestic flights.

Canadian Citizens:
Canadian citizens do not need a visa for stays up to 90 days for tourism or business purposes.

A valid passport is required for entry.

European Union Citizens:
>> Citizens of most European Union countries are eligible to travel to Hawaii under the Visa Waiver Program (VWP).
>> Under the VWP, travelers can stay for up to 90 days for tourism or business purposes without a visa.
>> However, VWP travelers MUST obtain an approved Electronic System for Travel Authorization (ESTA) before departure.

Other Nationalities:
>> Citizens of countries not participating in the VWP will generally need to obtain a B-2 tourist visa or a B-1 business visa before traveling to Hawaii.
>> Visa requirements vary depending on your country of citizenship. Check the U.S. embassy or consulate website for your country for specific instructions.

Electronic System for Travel Authorization (ESTA):
>> The ESTA is a mandatory travel authorization for VWP travelers.
>> You must apply for an ESTA online at least 72 hours before departure.
>> The ESTA is valid for multiple entries over two years or until your passport expires, whichever comes first.
>> There is a fee to apply for the ESTA.

COVID-19 Related Travel Restrictions:
>> Currently, there are no COVID-19 related travel restrictions for domestic travelers within the United States, including travel to Hawaii.
>> International travelers should check the latest travel advisories and requirements for entering the U.S. on the official websites of the U.S. Department of State and the Centers for Disease Control and Prevention (CDC).

Health & Safety

While Hawaii is a paradise destination, it's important to be aware of potential health and safety concerns and take precautions to ensure a safe and enjoyable trip.

Health:

>> Vaccinations: No specific vaccinations are required for travel to Hawaii from the U.S. mainland. However, it's always a good idea to be up-to-date on routine vaccinations like measles, mumps, rubella (MMR), diphtheria-tetanus-pertussis, chickenpox, polio, and your yearly flu shot.

>> Sun Protection: The Hawaiian sun is intense. Always wear sunscreen with SPF 30 or higher, a hat, and sunglasses. Seek shade during the hottest hours of the day.

>> Dehydration: Stay hydrated by drinking plenty of water, especially when spending time outdoors.

>> Ocean Safety: Pay attention to posted warning signs and flags at beaches. Never swim alone, and be cautious of strong currents and waves.

>> Jellyfish: Box jellyfish are present in Hawaiian waters, especially after full moons. Avoid swimming during those times or wear a protective rash guard.

>> Mosquitoes: Mosquito-borne illnesses are rare in Hawaii, but it's a good idea to use insect repellent, especially at dawn and dusk.

Safety:

>> Hiking Safety: Choose trails that match your fitness level and experience. Stay on marked trails, inform someone of your plans, and pack plenty of water and snacks.

>> Ocean Safety: Be aware of potential hazards like coral reefs, sharp rocks, and strong currents. Always swim at lifeguard-protected beaches.

>> Driving Safety: Familiarize yourself with Hawaii's traffic laws and road signs. Be extra cautious on winding roads and in wet conditions.

>> Valuables: Don't leave valuables unattended in your car or on the beach. Use hotel safes for important documents and expensive items.
>> Emergency Services: Dial 911 for police, fire, or medical emergencies.

Additional Tips:
>> Pack a first-aid kit with essentials like band-aids, pain relievers, and antihistamines.
>> Consider purchasing travel insurance to cover unexpected medical expenses or trip cancellations.
>> Be aware of your surroundings and trust your instincts. If something doesn't feel right, move to a safer location.
>> Familiarize yourself with local emergency procedures and evacuation routes in case of natural disasters like tsunamis or hurricanes.

Packing Tips for Both Islands

Packing efficiently for your Hawaiian getaway is key to maximizing enjoyment and minimizing hassle. With diverse climates and activities on both Oahu and the Big Island, it's important to strike the right balance between preparedness and packing light.

Essentials for Both Islands:
>> Swimwear: Pack multiple swimsuits for beach days and water activities.
>> Cover-Ups: Lightweight sarongs, dresses, or shirts to wear over your swimsuit.
>> Shorts and T-shirts: Comfortable clothes for daily wear and exploring.
>> Lightweight Pants or Skirts: For cooler evenings or dressier occasions.
>> Rain Jacket or Poncho: Hawaii's weather can change quickly, so be prepared for showers.
>> Hat and Sunglasses: Protect yourself from the strong Hawaiian sun.

>> Reef-Safe Sunscreen: Essential for protecting your skin and the delicate coral reefs.
>> Insect Repellent: Especially if you plan on hiking or spending time outdoors.
>> Comfortable Walking Shoes: For exploring towns, hiking trails, and volcanic landscapes.
>> Water Shoes or Sandals: For protecting your feet from sharp rocks and coral.
>> Snorkel Gear: If you plan on snorkeling, bring your own to avoid rental fees.
>> Reusable Water Bottle: Stay hydrated and reduce plastic waste.
>> Camera and Charger: Capture all the memories of your trip.
>> Travel Adapter: If you're traveling from outside the U.S.

Additional Tips for Oahu:
>> Dressier Attire: If you plan on experiencing the nightlife in Honolulu or Waikiki, pack a few dressier outfits.
>> Hiking Gear: If you want to tackle Oahu's hiking trails, pack sturdy shoes, a backpack, and plenty of water.

Additional Tips for the Big Island:
>> Warm Layers: Temperatures can drop significantly at higher elevations, especially in Volcanoes National Park.
>> Hiking Boots: Essential for exploring volcanic landscapes.
>> Long Pants and Sleeves: To protect yourself from sun and mosquitoes.
>> Headlamp or Flashlight: Helpful for exploring lava tubes or stargazing.

Packing Light:
>> Choose Versatile Pieces: Pack clothes that can be mixed and matched to create different outfits.
>> Stick to a Color Scheme: This will make it easier to create coordinated looks.
>> Utilize Laundry Facilities: Many hotels and vacation rentals have laundry facilities, allowing you to wash clothes and pack less.

>> Roll, Don't Fold: Rolling clothes can save space and prevent wrinkles.

>> Pack Toiletries in Travel-Sized Containers: Save space and avoid carrying bulky bottles.

Transportation on Oahu & Big Island

Major Car Rental Companies

National Brands

1️⃣ **Alamo**

📄 **Description:**

Alamo offers a wide range of vehicles at competitive prices, making it a popular choice for both leisure and business travelers. They provide an easy online booking system and various pick-up locations, especially convenient at airports.

🔨 **Location:** Various locations including major airports and city centers.

💳 **Prices:**

>> Economy: Starting at $30 per day

>> SUV: Starting at $50 per day

Pros and Cons:

Pros: Competitive pricing, extensive fleet, convenient locations

Cons: Additional fees for young drivers, high demand can lead to limited availability

Booking Website/Contact Details:

🌐 **Website:** www.alamo.com

☎ **Phone:** +1 800-462-5266

2 Avis

Description:

Avis is known for its excellent customer service and a wide selection of vehicles. They offer flexible rental options, including one-way rentals and long-term rentals.

Location: Available at major airports, downtown locations, and resort areas.

Prices:

» Compact: Starting at $35 per day
» Luxury: Starting at $70 per day

Pros and Cons:

Pros: High-quality customer service, wide range of vehicles, loyalty program

Cons: Higher prices compared to some competitors, additional fees for certain services

Booking Website/Contact Details:

Website: www.avis.com
Phone: +1 800-352-7900

3 Budget

Description:

Budget offers affordable rental options with a variety of vehicle choices. Ideal for budget-conscious travelers, they provide a straightforward rental process with optional add-ons.

Location: Locations include airports and city centers.

Prices:

» Economy: Starting at $25 per day
» Full-size: Starting at $45 per day

Pros and Cons:
Pros: Affordable rates, easy booking process, various discounts available
Cons: Limited luxury vehicle options, customer service can vary by location

Booking Website/Contact Details:
🌐 **Website:** www.budget.com
☎ **Phone:** +1 800-527-0700

4 Dollar
📄 **Description:**
Dollar Rent A Car is known for its budget-friendly rates and straightforward rental policies. They offer a range of vehicles suitable for families and budget travelers.

📍 **Location:** Primarily at airports and tourist areas.

🚌 **Prices:**
Compact: Starting at $28 per day
Minivan: Starting at $60 per day

Pros and Cons:
Pros: Low rates, family-friendly options, no hidden fees
Cons: Limited locations outside airports, basic customer service

Booking Website/Contact Details:
🌐 **Website:** www.dollar.com
☎ **Phone:** +1 800-800-4000

5 Enterprise
📄 **Description:**
Enterprise is well-regarded for its customer service and extensive network of locations, including many neighborhood locations in addition to airports. They offer a wide range of vehicles and flexible rental terms.

Location: Widespread, including airports and local branches.

Prices:
>> Economy: Starting at $30 per day
>> SUV: Starting at $55 per day

Pros and Cons:
Pros: Excellent customer service, extensive location network, various vehicle options
Cons: Can be pricier than some competitors, additional fees may apply

Booking Website/Contact Details:
Website: www.enterprise.com
Phone: +1 855-266-9289

6 Hertz
Description:
Hertz offers a premium rental experience with a wide range of vehicles, including luxury and specialty cars. They provide excellent service and a comprehensive rewards program.

Location: Available at airports, city centers, and various locations worldwide.

Prices:
>> Compact: Starting at $35 per day
>> Luxury: Starting at $80 per day

Pros and Cons:
Pros: High-quality vehicles, extensive rewards program, premium customer service
Cons: Higher prices, additional fees for premium services

Booking Website/Contact Details:

🌐 **Website:** www.hertz.com

☎ **Phone:** +1 800-654-3131

---

⑦ National
📑 **Description:**

National Car Rental is a popular choice for business travelers, offering a wide selection of vehicles and quick pick-up and drop-off services. Their Emerald Club loyalty program is highly rated.

🗝 **Location:** Mainly at airports and major cities.

💳 **Prices:**

» Midsize: Starting at $40 per day

» Full-size: Starting at $50 per day

Pros and Cons:

Pros: Efficient service, excellent loyalty program, wide range of vehicles

Cons: Higher prices, fewer discounts available

Booking Website/Contact Details:

🌐 **Website:** www.nationalcar.com

☎ **Phone:** +1 844-393-9989

---

⑧ Thrifty
📑 **Description:**

Thrifty offers budget-friendly rental options with a focus on value. They provide a range of vehicles that cater to budget-conscious travelers.

🗝 **Location:** Primarily at airports and key tourist destinations.

Prices:
>> Economy: Starting at $27 per day
>> SUV: Starting at $55 per day

Pros and Cons:
Pros: Affordable rates, straightforward rental process, various discounts
Cons: Limited luxury options, customer service varies by location

Booking Website/Contact Details:
🌐 **Website:** www.thrifty.com
☎ **Phone:** +1 800-847-4389

Local Companies

① Lucky Owl Car Rental
📝 **Description:**
Lucky Owl Car Rental is a local company known for its friendly service and affordable rates. They offer a range of vehicles, including older models, which helps keep costs down.

🔨 **Location:** Honolulu, HI

Prices:
>> Economy: Starting at $25 per day
>> SUV: Starting at $45 per day

Pros and Cons:
Pros: Affordable rates, friendly service, flexible rental terms
Cons: Limited locations, older vehicle models

Booking Website/Contact Details:
🌐 **Website:** www.luckyowl.com
☎ **Phone:** +1 808-352-4890

2 808 Smart Car Rentals

Description:

808 Smart Car Rentals offers a fleet of compact and fuel-efficient vehicles, ideal for navigating the island with ease. They focus on providing excellent customer service and competitive pricing.

Location: Honolulu, HI

Prices:

Smart Car: Starting at $30 per day

Pros and Cons:

Pros: Fuel-efficient vehicles, easy parking, competitive rates
Cons: Limited to compact cars, fewer vehicle options

Booking Website/Contact Details:

Website: www.808smartcarrentals.com
Phone: +1 808-800-2277

3 Advantage Rent-a-Car

Description:

Advantage Rent-a-Car offers a range of vehicles at competitive prices. They focus on providing straightforward rental services without the extra fees often found with larger companies.

Location: Honolulu, HI

Prices:

>> Economy: Starting at $25 per day
>> Full-size: Starting at $45 per day

Pros and Cons:

Pros: Competitive rates, straightforward rental process, no hidden fees
Cons: Limited locations, basic customer service

Booking Website/Contact Details:

🌐 **Website:** www.advantage.com

☎ **Phone:** +1 800-777-5500

Information for Decision Making:
Location:
>> Most companies have counters at the major airports (HNL, KOA, ITO) and in popular tourist areas like Waikiki.
>> Consider your arrival airport and planned destinations to choose a convenient pickup location.

Vehicle Selection:
>> Economy cars are the most affordable option, suitable for couples or solo travelers.
>> SUVs and minivans are ideal for families or groups with lots of luggage.
>> Convertibles offer a fun way to enjoy the scenery, but book early as they're popular.

Rates & Fees:
>> Compare rates online or through a travel agent to find the best deals.
>> Be aware of additional fees, such as taxes, airport surcharges, underage driver fees, and optional insurance.

Insurance:
>> Check if your personal car insurance or credit card covers rental car insurance.
>> If not, consider purchasing the rental company's insurance or independent coverage.

Reservation Policies:
>> Book in advance, especially during peak season, to ensure availability and lock in rates.
>> Understand the cancellation and refund policies of the rental company.

- ›› Driver's License & Age Requirements:
- ›› You'll need a valid driver's license from your home country.
- ›› Some companies have minimum age requirements (typically 21 or 25).

Additional Drivers:
- ›› Check if there are fees for adding additional drivers to your rental agreement.

Fuel Policy:
- ›› Most companies offer the option to prepay for a full tank of gas or return the car with a full tank.

Customer Service:
- ›› Read online reviews to get an idea of the company's reputation for customer service.

Tips for Choosing a Car Rental Company

Compare Prices: Use comparison websites to compare rates from different companies.

Read Reviews: Check online reviews to see what other travelers have experienced.

Consider Your Needs: Choose a company with a location and vehicle selection that suits your needs.

Factor in Fees: Don't forget to factor in additional fees like taxes and insurance when comparing prices.

Book Early: Reserve your rental car well in advance, especially during peak season.

Tipping & Etiquette

Tipping and etiquette play a significant role in Hawaiian culture, reflecting the islands' values of respect, hospitality, and aloha spirit. Understanding these customs will help you navigate social interactions smoothly and show appreciation for the services you receive.

Tipping:

While tipping is not mandatory in Hawaii, it is customary and appreciated in many service industries. Here's a general guideline for tipping:

>> Restaurants: 15-20% of the total bill is standard for good service. If you're dining with a large group (6 or more), check if gratuity is automatically added to the bill.
>> Bars: $1-2 per drink or 15-20% of the total tab.

Hotel Staff:

>> Bellhop: $1-2 per bag
>> Housekeeping: $2-5 per night
>> Concierge: $5-10 for exceptional service
>> Tour Guides and Drivers: $5-10 per person is customary for a good experience.
>> Valet Parking: $2-5 when you pick up your car.
>> Taxis: 15-20% of the fare.

Remember: Tipping is a personal choice, and you can adjust the amount based on the quality of service you receive.

Etiquette:

>> Beyond tipping, here are some etiquette tips to keep in mind:
>> Greetings: "Aloha" is a versatile greeting that can mean hello, goodbye, or love.
>> Removing Shoes: It's customary to remove your shoes before entering someone's home or certain establishments like temples or hula halls.
>> Respect for Nature: Hawaii's natural beauty is cherished. Avoid leaving trash on beaches or trails, and be respectful of wildlife and marine life.
>> Aloha Spirit: Embrace the aloha spirit of kindness, hospitality, and respect for others. Say "mahalo" (thank you) often, and be patient and understanding in all interactions.

>> Learn a Few Hawaiian Words: Even a few phrases like "mahalo" (thank you), "aloha" (hello/goodbye), and "maika'i" (good) can go a long way in showing respect for the local culture.

Additional Tips:

>> Be aware of your surroundings and respect private property.

>> When visiting sacred sites or cultural attractions, dress modestly and follow any posted rules.

>> If you're unsure about tipping or etiquette in a particular situation, don't hesitate to ask a local for guidance.

ITINERARIES: JOURNEY MADE EASY

Hoomaluhia Botanical Garden

3-day Itinerary

Day 1: Exploring Honolulu and Waikiki (Oahu)

🖵 Morning: Diamond Head State Monument

⮕ **Time:** 8:00 AM - 10:00 AM

Activity: Start your day with a hike up Diamond Head for panoramic views of Honolulu and the Pacific Ocean. The hike is moderately challenging but well worth the effort.

🗡 **Location:** Diamond Head Road, Honolulu, HI 96815

Rest/Dining: After the hike, grab a refreshing smoothie or acai bowl from Bogart's Cafe, located nearby.

🖵 Mid-Morning: Waikiki Beach

⮕ **Time:** 10:30 AM - 12:30 PM

Activity: Head to Waikiki Beach to relax on the sandy shores, swim, or try some surfing lessons.

🗡 **Location:** Waikiki Beach, Honolulu, HI 96815

Rest/Dining: Enjoy a light lunch at Duke's Waikiki, famous for its beachfront views and Hawaiian cuisine.

◯ Afternoon: Iolani Palace and Downtown Honolulu

⮕ **Time:** 1:30 PM - 4:00 PM

Activity: Explore Iolani Palace, the only royal palace in the United States, and take a walk around downtown Honolulu to see historical sites.

🗡 **Location:** 364 S King St, Honolulu, HI 96813

Rest/Dining: Stop for a coffee and a snack at The Nook Neighborhood Bistro.

🏙 Evening: Waikiki Strip

⮕ **Time:** 6:00 PM - 9:00 PM

Activity: Stroll along the Waikiki Strip, shop at the boutiques, and enjoy the lively atmosphere. Watch the sunset from the beach.

🗡 **Location:** Kalakaua Avenue, Honolulu, HI 96815

Rest/Dining: Have dinner at Marukame Udon, a popular spot for delicious and affordable udon noodles.

Day 2: North Shore and Cultural Experiences (Oahu)

🖵 Morning: Dole Plantation
➭ **Time:** 9:00 AM - 11:00 AM
Activity: Visit the Dole Plantation to learn about Hawaii's pineapple history, take a train tour, and try the famous Dole Whip.
🖎 **Location:** 64-1550 Kamehameha Hwy, Wahiawa, HI 96786
Rest/Dining: Enjoy a mid-morning snack at the Pineapple Grille within the plantation.

🖵 Mid-Morning: Waimea Valley
➭ **Time:** 11:30 AM - 1:30 PM
Activity: Explore the botanical gardens and historical sites of Waimea Valley, ending with a swim at Waimea Falls.
🖎 **Location:** 59-864 Kamehameha Hwy, Haleiwa, HI 96712
Rest/Dining: Have lunch at the Waimea Valley Grill, offering fresh and local options.

○ Afternoon: North Shore Beaches
➭ **Time:** 2:00 PM - 5:00 PM
Activity: Spend the afternoon at famous North Shore beaches like Sunset Beach and Banzai Pipeline, perfect for watching surfers.
🖎 **Location:** North Shore, Oahu, HI
Rest/Dining: Stop by Ted's Bakery for a slice of their famous pie.

🏢 Evening: Polynesian Cultural Center
➭ **Time:** 6:00 PM - 9:00 PM
Activity: Experience the Polynesian Cultural Center with cultural shows, village tours, and a luau dinner.
🖎 **Location:** 55-370 Kamehameha Hwy, Laie, HI 96762
Rest/Dining: Enjoy the included dinner at the center's luau.

Day 3: Hilo and Volcanoes National Park (Big Island)

Morning: Rainbow Falls and Lili'uokalani Gardens
⇨ **Time:** 8:00 AM - 10:00 AM
Activity: Start your day with a visit to Rainbow Falls, followed by a peaceful stroll through Lili'uokalani Gardens.
Location: Rainbow Falls, Hilo, HI 96720; Lili'uokalani Gardens, Banyan Dr, Hilo, HI 96720
Rest/Dining: Have breakfast at Ken's House of Pancakes, a local favorite.

Mid-Morning: Akaka Falls State Park
⇨ **Time:** 10:30 AM - 12:00 PM
Activity: Explore the lush trails leading to Akaka Falls, a stunning 442-foot waterfall.
Location: 875 Akaka Falls Rd, Honomu, HI 96728
Rest/Dining: Enjoy a snack from a local vendor at the park entrance.

Afternoon: Hawaii Volcanoes National Park
⇨ **Time:** 1:00 PM - 4:00 PM
Activity: Discover the unique landscapes of Hawaii Volcanoes National Park. Visit the Kilauea Visitor Center, Thurston Lava Tube, and take a walk on the Devastation Trail.
Location: Hawaii Volcanoes National Park, HI 96718
Rest/Dining: Have lunch at Volcano House Restaurant, offering views of the crater.

Evening: Hilo Downtown and Banyan Drive
⇨ **Time:** 5:00 PM - 8:00 PM
Activity: Explore downtown Hilo, visit local shops, and stroll along Banyan Drive.
Location: Hilo, HI
Rest/Dining: Enjoy dinner at Cafe Pesto, known for its island-inspired dishes.

7-day Itinerary

Day 1: Exploring Honolulu and Waikiki (Oahu)

Morning: Diamond Head State Monument

➡ **Time:** 8:00 AM - 10:00 AM
Activity: Hike up Diamond Head for panoramic views.
📍 **Location:** Diamond Head Road, Honolulu, HI 96815
Rest/Dining: Bogart's Cafe

Mid-Morning: Waikiki Beach

➡ **Time:** 10:30 AM - 12:30 PM
Activity: Relax or surf at Waikiki Beach.
📍 **Location:** Waikiki Beach, Honolulu, HI 96815
Rest/Dining: Duke's Waikiki

Afternoon: Iolani Palace and Downtown Honolulu

➡ **Time:** 1:30 PM - 4:00 PM
Activity: Explore Iolani Palace and downtown.
📍 **Location:** 364 S King St, Honolulu, HI 96813
Rest/Dining: The Nook Neighborhood Bistro

Evening: Waikiki Strip

➡ **Time:** 6:00 PM - 9:00 PM
Activity: Stroll and shop along Waikiki Strip.
📍 **Location:** Kalakaua Avenue, Honolulu, HI 96815
Rest/Dining: Marukame Udon

Day 2: North Shore and Cultural Experiences (Oahu)

Morning: Dole Plantation

➡ **Time:** 9:00 AM - 11:00 AM
Activity: Visit and tour the Dole Plantation.
📍 **Location:** 64-1550 Kamehameha Hwy, Wahiawa, HI 96786
Rest/Dining: Pineapple Grille

⬛ Mid-Morning: Waimea Valley
➡ **Time:** 11:30 AM - 1:30 PM
Activity: Explore Waimea Valley and Falls.
⚜ **Location:** 59-864 Kamehameha Hwy, Haleiwa, HI 96712
Rest/Dining: Waimea Valley Grill

⬤ Afternoon: North Shore Beaches
➡ **Time:** 2:00 PM - 5:00 PM
Activity: Visit Sunset Beach and Banzai Pipeline.
⚜ **Location:** North Shore, Oahu, HI
Rest/Dining: Ted's Bakery

▦ Evening: Polynesian Cultural Center
➡ **Time:** 6:00 PM - 9:00 PM
Activity: Enjoy cultural shows and a luau.
⚜ **Location:** 55-370 Kamehameha Hwy, Laie, HI 96762
Rest/Dining: Polynesian Cultural Center Luau

Day 3: Hilo and Volcanoes National Park (Big Island)

⬛ Morning: Rainbow Falls and Lili'uokalani Gardens
➡ **Time:** 8:00 AM - 10:00 AM
Activity: Visit Rainbow Falls and Lili'uokalani Gardens.
⚜ **Location:** Hilo, HI
Rest/Dining: Ken's House of Pancakes

⬛ Mid-Morning: Akaka Falls State Park
➡ **Time:** 10:30 AM - 12:00 PM
Activity: Explore Akaka Falls.
⚜ **Location:** 875 Akaka Falls Rd, Honomu, HI 96728
Rest/Dining: Local vendor snacks

○ Afternoon: Hawaii Volcanoes National Park

⇨ **Time:** 1:00 PM - 4:00 PM

Activity: Discover Volcanoes National Park.

⚒ **Location:** Hawaii Volcanoes National Park, HI 96718

Rest/Dining: Volcano House Restaurant

▦ Evening: Hilo Downtown and Banyan Drive

⇨ **Time:** 5:00 PM - 8:00 PM

Activity: Explore downtown Hilo.

⚒ **Location:** Hilo, HI

Rest/Dining: Cafe Pesto

Day 4: Kona Coast and Historical Sites (Big Island)

▣ Morning: Puʻuhonua o Hōnaunau National Historical Park

⇨ **Time:** 8:00 AM - 10:00 AM

Activity: Visit the Place of Refuge.

⚒ **Location:** 1871 Trail, Honaunau, HI 96726

Rest/Dining: Local snack bar

▣ Mid-Morning: Kona Coffee Living History Farm

⇨ **Time:** 10:30 AM - 12:00 PM

Activity: Tour the coffee farm.

⚒ **Location:** 82-6199 Mamalahoa Hwy, Captain Cook, HI 96704

Rest/Dining: Coffee tasting

○ Afternoon: Kealakekua Bay

⇨ **Time:** 1:00 PM - 3:00 PM

Activity: Snorkel in Kealakekua Bay.

⚒ **Location:** Kealakekua, HI 96750

Rest/Dining: Picnic lunch

Evening: Kailua-Kona
➡ **Time:** 4:00 PM - 7:00 PM
Activity: Explore Kailua-Kona town.
Location: Kailua-Kona, HI
Rest/Dining: Huggo's on the Rocks

Day 5: Waimea and Kohala Coast (Big Island)

Morning: Waimea Town and Parker Ranch
➡ **Time:** 8:00 AM - 10:00 AM
Activity: Explore Waimea and visit Parker Ranch.
Location: Waimea, HI
Rest/Dining: Hawaiian Style Cafe

Mid-Morning: Pololu Valley Lookout
➡ **Time:** 10:30 AM - 12:00 PM
Activity: Hike and explore Pololu Valley.
Location: North Kohala, HI
Rest/Dining: Picnic with scenic views

Afternoon: Hawi Town
➡ **Time:** 1:00 PM - 3:00 PM
Activity: Discover the charming town of Hawi.
Location: Hawi, HI
Rest/Dining: Bamboo Restaurant

Evening: Hapuna Beach
➡ **Time:** 4:00 PM - 7:00 PM
Activity: Relax and swim at Hapuna Beach.
Location: Kohala Coast, HI
Rest/Dining: Sunset picnic

Day 6: Hanauma Bay and East Oahu (Oahu)

Morning: Hanauma Bay
Time: 8:00 AM - 10:30 AM
Activity: Snorkel in Hanauma Bay.
Location: 7455 Kalaniana'ole Hwy, Honolulu, HI 96825
Rest/Dining: Snack bar at Hanauma Bay

Mid-Morning: Makapu'u Point Lighthouse Trail
Time: 11:00 AM - 12:30 PM
Activity: Hike to the lighthouse for stunning views.
Location: 8751-905 Kalaniana'ole Hwy, Honolulu, HI 96825
Rest/Dining: Pack snacks and water

Afternoon: Waimanalo Beach
Time: 1:00 PM - 3:00 PM
Activity: Relax and swim at Waimanalo Beach.
Location: Waimanalo Beach, HI
Rest/Dining: Ono Steaks and Shrimp Shack

Evening: Kailua Town
Time: 4:00 PM - 7:00 PM
Activity: Explore Kailua town and Lanikai Beach.
Location: Kailua, HI
Rest/Dining: Buzz's Original Steak House

Day 7: Culture and Adventure in Honolulu (Oahu)

Morning: Pearl Harbor National Memorial
Time: 8:00 AM - 11:00 AM
Activity: Visit the USS Arizona Memorial and Pearl Harbor sites.
Location: 1 Arizona Memorial Place, Honolulu, HI 96818
Rest/Dining: Visitor center snack bar

🖥 Mid-Morning: **Bishop Museum**

➡ **Time:** 11:30 AM - 1:00 PM

Activity: Explore Hawaiian history and culture.

🏹 **Location:** 1525 Bernice St, Honolulu, HI 96817

Rest/Dining: Museum cafe

☼ Afternoon: **Ala Moana Center**

➡ **Time:** 2:00 PM - 4:00 PM

Activity: Shop and dine at Ala Moana Center.

🏹 **Location:** 1450 Ala Moana Blvd, Honolulu, HI 96814

Rest/Dining: Food court with diverse options

🏙 Evening: **Sunset Dinner Cruise**

➡ **Time:** 5:00 PM - 8:00 PM

Activity: Enjoy a sunset dinner cruise along the coast.

🏹 **Location:** Departure from Honolulu Harbor

Rest/Dining: Dinner included on the cruise

APPENDICES

Hawaiian Basic Phrases

Basic Phrases

>> *Hello / Goodbye*
Aloha (ah-LOH-hah)
A versatile greeting used to say hello and goodbye, reflecting love and affection.

>> *Thank You*
Mahalo (mah-HAH-loh)
Used to express gratitude and appreciation.

>> *Yes*
'Ae (ah-EH)
Simple affirmation meaning yes.

>> *No*
'A'ole (ah-OH-leh)
Simple negation meaning no.

>> *Please*
E 'olu'olu (eh OH-loo OH-loo)
Used to politely request something.

>> *Excuse Me / I'm Sorry*
E kala mai ia'u (eh KAH-lah my ee-AH-oo)
Used to apologize or ask for pardon.

>> *You're Welcome*
'A'ole pilikia (ah-OH-leh pee-lee-KEE-ah)
Means no problem or you're welcome in response to thanks.

Greetings

>> *Good Morning*
Aloha kakahiaka (ah-LOH-hah kah-kah-hee-AH-kah)
Used to wish someone a good morning.

>> *Good Afternoon*
Aloha 'auinalā (ah-LOH-hah ow-ee-nah-LAH)
Used to wish someone a good afternoon.

>> *Good Evening*
Aloha ahiahi (ah-LOH-hah ah-hee-AH-hee)
Used to wish someone a good evening.

>> *Good Night*
Aloha pō (ah-LOH-hah poh)
Used to wish someone a good night.

>> *Welcome*
E komo mai (eh KOH-moh my)
Used to welcome someone warmly.

Common Questions

>> *How are you?*
Pehea 'oe? (peh-HEH-ah oh-EH)
A common way to ask someone how they are.

>> *What is your name?*
'O wai kou inoa? (oh vie koh ee-NOH-ah)
Used to ask someone's name.

>> *Where are you from?*
No hea mai 'oe? (noh HEH-ah my oh-EH)
Used to ask someone's place of origin.

>> *How much does it cost?*
'Ehia ka uku? (eh-HEE-ah kah oo-KOO)
Used to inquire about the price of something.

>> *Where is the bathroom?*
Ma hea ka lumi ho'opau pilikia? (mah HEH-ah kah LOO-mee hoh-oh-PAH-oo pee-lee-KEE-ah)
Used to ask for the location of the restroom.

Courtesy Phrases

>> *Thank you very much*
Mahalo nui loa (mah-HAH-loh NOO-ee LOH-ah)
Used to express deep gratitude.

>> *Sorry for the inconvenience*
Ke kala nui ia'u (keh KAH-lah NOO-ee ee-AH-oo)
Used to apologize for causing trouble.

>> *Excuse me (getting attention)*
E kala mai (eh KAH-lah my)
Used to politely get someone's attention.

Directions

>> *Left*
Hema (HEH-mah)
Used to indicate direction to the left.

>> *Right*
'Akau (ah-KOW)
Used to indicate direction to the right.

>> *Straight ahead*
Pololei (poh-loh-LAY)
Used to indicate to go straight ahead.

>> *Stop*
Kū (KOO)
Used to instruct someone to stop.

Expressions of Time

>> *Now*
'Ānō (AH-noh)
Indicates the present moment.

>> *Later*
Ma hope (mah HOH-peh)
Indicates a later time.

>> *Today*
I kēia lā (ee KEH-ee-ah LAH)
Refers to the current day.

>> *Tomorrow*
'Apōpō (ah-POH-poh)
Refers to the following day.

>> *Yesterday*
Inanahi (ee-NAH-nah-hee)
Refers to the day before today.

Travel and Transportation

>> *Airport*
Kahua mokulele (kah-HOO-ah moh-koo-LEH-leh)
The Hawaiian word for airport.

>> *Bus*
Ka'a 'ōhua (KAH-ah OH-hoo-ah)
The Hawaiian word for bus.

>> *Car*
Ka'a (KAH-ah)
The Hawaiian word for car.

>> *Taxi*
Ka'a lawe 'ōhua (KAH-ah LAH-veh OH-hoo-ah)
The Hawaiian phrase for taxi.

>> *Ticket*
Kāleka ho'okomo (KAH-leh-kah hoh-oh-KOH-moh)
The Hawaiian phrase for ticket.

Food and Dining

>> *Food*
'Ai (ah-EE)
The general term for food.

>> *Water*
Wai (why)
The Hawaiian word for water.

>> *Delicious*
'Ono (OH-noh)
Used to describe tasty food.

>> *Restaurant*
Hale 'aina (HAH-leh EYE-nah)
The Hawaiian term for restaurant.

>> *Menu*
Pāpā 'aina (PAH-pah EYE-nah)
The Hawaiian phrase for menu.

>> *Bill / Check*
Palapala 'ai (PAH-lah-PAH-lah ah-EE)
Used to ask for the bill in a restaurant.

Emergency

>> *Help!*
Kōkua! (KOH-koo-ah)
A call for help in an emergency.

>> *Call the police*
Kāhea i ka māka'i (KAH-heh-ah ee kah MAH-kah-ee)
Used to request police assistance.

>> *Fire*
Ahi (AH-hee)

The Hawaiian word for fire, used in emergencies.

>> *Doctor*
Kauka (KOW-kah)
The Hawaiian word for doctor.

>> *Hospital*
Hale ma'i (HAH-leh MAH-ee)
The Hawaiian term for hospital.

Weather

>> *Sunny*
Lā (lah)
Refers to sunny weather.
>> *Rainy*
Ua (oo-AH)
Refers to rainy weather.
>> *Cloudy*

Ao (ow)
Indicates cloudy skies.
>> *Windy*
Makani (mah-KAH-nee)
Refers to windy conditions.
>> *Hot*
Wela (WEH-lah)
Describes hot weather.

Oahu & Big Island Maps

Apps

Google Maps
📄 **Description:** Comprehensive navigation app offering driving, walking, and transit directions. Includes real-time traffic updates, street view, and satellite imagery.
Download: Available on Google Play and App Store.

Maps.me
📄 **Description:** Offline maps app with detailed maps and navigation. Great for exploring remote areas without internet.
Download: Available on Google Play and App Store.

CityMaps2Go
📄 **Description:** Offers detailed offline maps and travel guides. Useful for exploring cities and planning itineraries.
Download: Available on Google Play and App Store.

Go Hawaii
📄 **Description:** Official tourism site offering detailed maps and guides for Oahu and the Big Island. Includes attractions, accommodations, and dining options.
🌐 **Website:** www.gohawaii.com

Hawaii Guide

📄 **Description:** Provides detailed maps and travel guides for all Hawaiian Islands. Includes information on attractions, accommodations, and activities.

🌐 **Website:** www.hawaii-guide.com

Big Island Hawaii Travel Guide

📄 **Description:** Detailed travel guides and maps specifically for the Big Island. Includes recommendations for activities, dining, and accommodations.

🌐 **Website:** www.lovebigisland.com

Downloadable PDF Maps

Oahu Visitors Bureau

📄 **Description:** Offers downloadable PDF maps of Oahu, highlighting key attractions, beaches, and accommodations.

🌐 **Website:** www.visit-oahu.com

Big Island Visitors Bureau

📄 **Description:** Provides detailed PDF maps of the Big Island, including points of interest, hiking trails, and accommodation options.

🌐 **Website:** www.gohawaii.com/islands/hawaii-big-island

National Park Service

📄 **Description:** Downloadable maps for Hawaii Volcanoes National Park, including hiking trails and visitor center locations.

🌐 **Website:** www.nps.gov/havo/planyourvisit/maps.htm

Hawaiian Islands

📄 **Description:** Offers comprehensive downloadable PDF maps of all Hawaiian Islands, including Oahu and the Big Island. Includes detailed road maps and attraction highlights.

🌐 **Website:** www.hawaiianislands.com

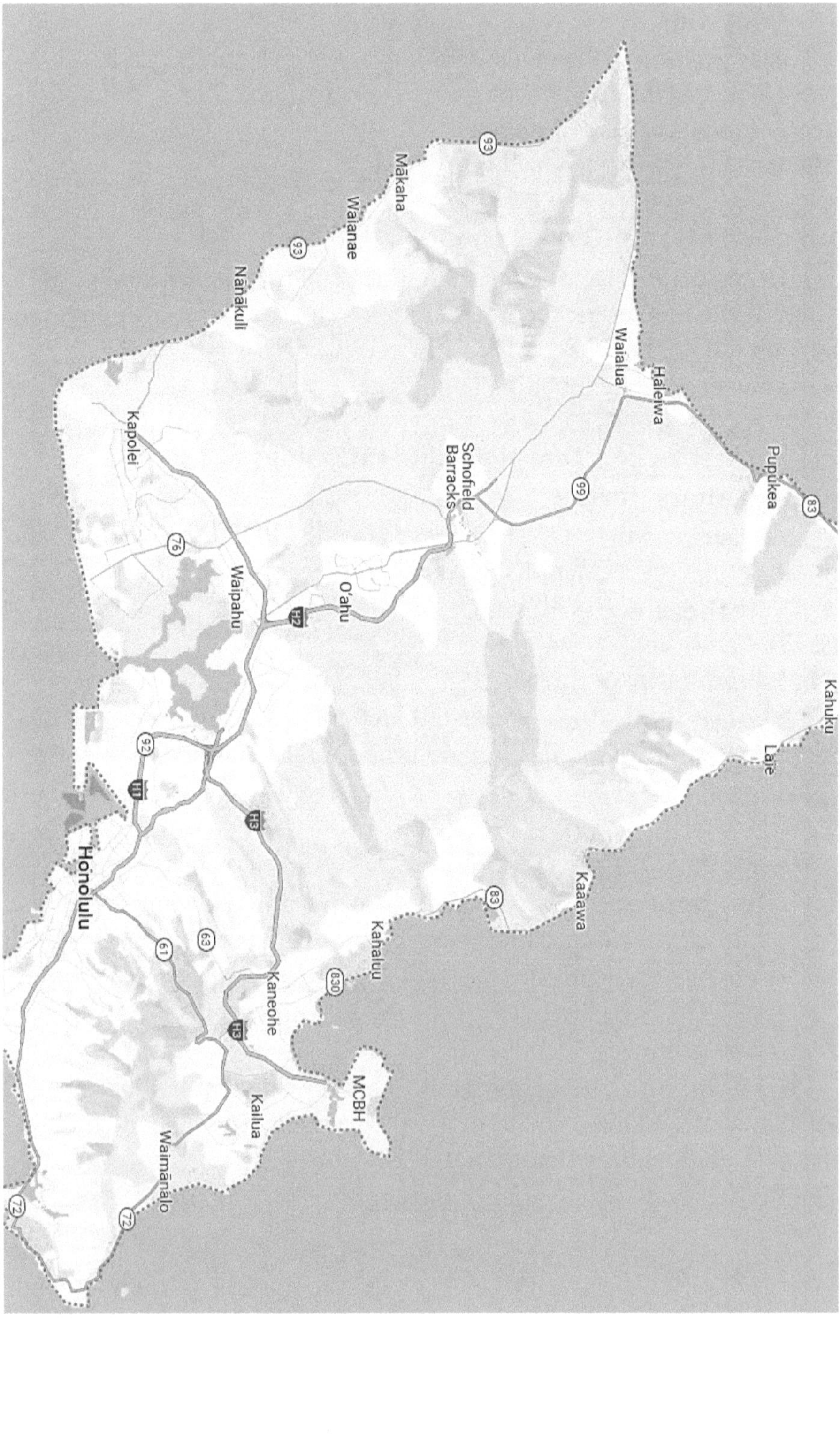
Mākaha
Waianae
Nānākuli
Kapolei
Waipahu
O'ahu
Schofield Barracks
Waialua
Haleiwa
Pupukea
Kahuku
Laie
Kaaawa
Kahaluu
Kaneohe
MCBH
Kailua
Waimānalo
Honolulu
93
99
83
76
H2
92
H1
H3
61
63
830
72

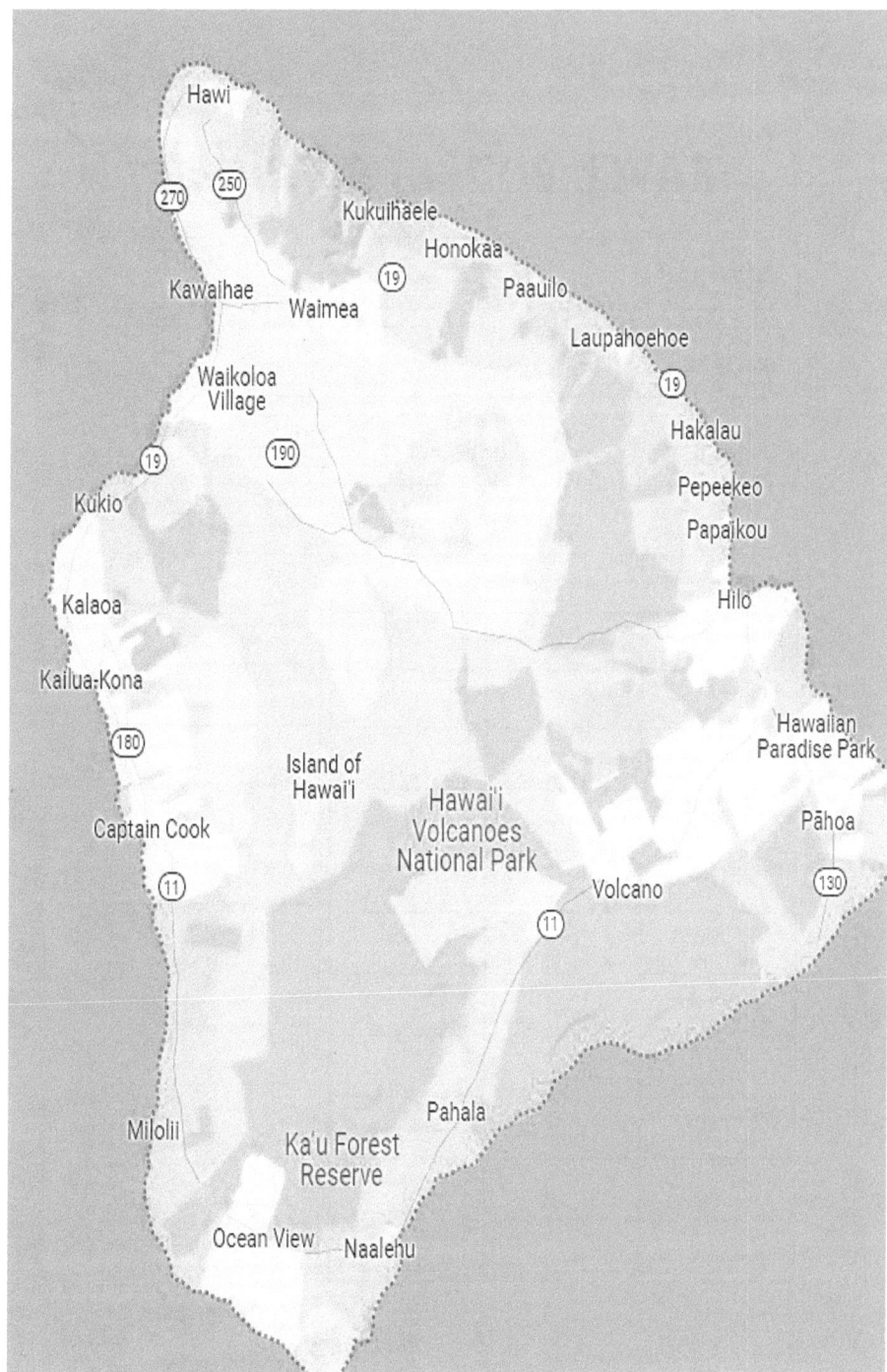

Hawi

270 250

Kukuihaele

Honokaa

Kawaihae   Waimea   19   Paauilo

Laupahoehoe

Waikoloa
Village   19

190   Hakalau

19   Pepeekeo

Kukio   Papaikou

Kalaoa   Hilo

Kailua-Kona

Hawaiian
Paradise Park

180

Island of
Hawai'i   Hawai'i
Volcanoes
National Park   Pāhoa

Captain Cook

11   130

Volcano

11

Pahala

Milolii   Ka'u Forest
Reserve

Ocean View   Naalehu

TRAVEL BUDGET PLANNER

DESTINATION:

TRAVEL DATES:

☐ VISA ☐ INSURANCE ☐ VACCINES

DETAIL	BUDGET	ACTUAL	NOTES
Visa Fee			
Insurance			
Airfare			
Hotel			
Train Tickets			
Bus Tickets			
Entrance Fee			
Food/Snacks			
Souvenirs			
Tours			
Drinks			
Extras			

TRAVEL BUDGET PLANNER

DESTINATION:

TRAVEL DATES:

☐ VISA   ☐ INSURANCE   ☐ VACCINES

DETAIL	BUDGET	ACTUAL	NOTES
Visa Fee			
Insurance			
Airfare			
Hotel			
Train Tickets			
Bus Tickets			
Entrance Fee			
Food/Snacks			
Souvenirs			
Tours			
Drinks			
Extras			

TRAVEL BUDGET PLANNER

DESTINATION:

TRAVEL DATES:

☐ VISA   ☐ INSURANCE   ☐ VACCINES

DETAIL	BUDGET	ACTUAL	NOTES
Visa Fee			
Insurance			
Airfare			
Hotel			
Train Tickets			
Bus Tickets			
Entrance Fee			
Food/Snacks			
Souvenirs			
Tours			
Drinks			
Extras			

TRAVEL BUDGET PLANNER

DESTINATION:

TRAVEL DATES:

☐ VISA   ☐ INSURANCE   ☐ VACCINES

DETAIL	BUDGET	ACTUAL	NOTES
Visa Fee			
Insurance			
Airfare			
Hotel			
Train Tickets			
Bus Tickets			
Entrance Fee			
Food/Snacks			
Souvenirs			
Tours			
Drinks			
Extras			

TRAVEL BUDGET PLANNER

DESTINATION:

TRAVEL DATES:

☐ VISA   ☐ INSURANCE   ☐ VACCINES

DETAIL	BUDGET	ACTUAL	NOTES
Visa Fee			
Insurance			
Airfare			
Hotel			
Train Tickets			
Bus Tickets			
Entrance Fee			
Food/Snacks			
Souvenirs			
Tours			
Drinks			
Extras			

TRAVEL BUDGET PLANNER

DESTINATION:

TRAVEL DATES:

☐ VISA   ☐ INSURANCE   ☐ VACCINES

DETAIL	BUDGET	ACTUAL	NOTES
Visa Fee			
Insurance			
Airfare			
Hotel			
Train Tickets			
Bus Tickets			
Entrance Fee			
Food/Snacks			
Souvenirs			
Tours			
Drinks			
Extras			

TRAVEL BUDGET PLANNER

DESTINATION:

TRAVEL DATES:

☐ VISA ☐ INSURANCE ☐ VACCINES

DETAIL	BUDGET	ACTUAL	NOTES
Visa Fee			
Insurance			
Airfare			
Hotel			
Train Tickets			
Bus Tickets			
Entrance Fee			
Food/Snacks			
Souvenirs			
Tours			
Drinks			
Extras			

TRAVEL BUDGET PLANNER

DESTINATION:

TRAVEL DATES:

☐ VISA ☐ INSURANCE ☐ VACCINES

DETAIL	BUDGET	ACTUAL	NOTES
Visa Fee			
Insurance			
Airfare			
Hotel			
Train Tickets			
Bus Tickets			
Entrance Fee			
Food/Snacks			
Souvenirs			
Tours			
Drinks			
Extras			

TRAVEL BUDGET PLANNER

DESTINATION:

TRAVEL DATES:

☐ VISA   ☐ INSURANCE   ☐ VACCINES

DETAIL	BUDGET	ACTUAL	NOTES
Visa Fee			
Insurance			
Airfare			
Hotel			
Train Tickets			
Bus Tickets			
Entrance Fee			
Food/Snacks			
Souvenirs			
Tours			
Drinks			
Extras			

TRAVEL BUDGET PLANNER

DESTINATION:

TRAVEL DATES:

☐ VISA   ☐ INSURANCE   ☐ VACCINES

DETAIL	BUDGET	ACTUAL	NOTES
Visa Fee			
Insurance			
Airfare			
Hotel			
Train Tickets			
Bus Tickets			
Entrance Fee			
Food/Snacks			
Souvenirs			
Tours			
Drinks			
Extras			

Made in United States
Troutdale, OR
03/10/2025